1 Introduction

The years leading to the 2007-2009 financial turmoil in the United States were characterized by the development of a new set of financial institutions that formed the so-called "shadow banking" (SB) system. A precise and all-encompassing definition of shadow banking is difficult to obtain, but it can broadly be characterized as a network of financial subjects that replicated the credit intermediation process by decomposing it in different activities while heavily relying on securitization and sophisticated financial products.[1]

These entities included, for example, broker-dealers, mortgage finance firms, asset-backed commercial paper (ABCP) conduits and money market mutual funds (MMMF), and provided an alternative chain of intermediation, parallel to the "traditional banking" (TB) offered by conventional banks. Simplifying considerably the complex structure of the shadow banking system, we can provide an example of the basic steps of the intermediation process as follows. Loans originated by non-bank lenders were pooled through securitization by a loan warehouse vehicle, for example a special purpose vehicle (SPV) supported by a broker-dealer.[2] The broker-dealer further combined such loans into structured asset backed securities (ABS) that were funded by issuing risk-free short term debt like commercial paper. MMMFs purchased the ABCP and financed themselves with money-like securities with stable net-asset value. As a result, we can think of the aggregate shadow banking system as engaging in the same maturity and liquidity transformation typical of traditional banks, converting illiquid loans into demandable instruments.

If, on the one hand, this financial system increased the amount of credit available to borrowers, on the other hand it proved to be inherently more fragile because of a series of risks affecting its business model. In this paper, I will focus on the following factors that increased the instability of the shadow banking system: high leverage, moral hazard in selecting the riskiness of loans, and exposure to bank runs. In addition, this paper will show how these channels can be amplified by the interaction with traditional banks, which are characterized by a lower leverage capacity.

Shadow banking, became more and more important in the years leading to the crisis. By 2007 the SB-system was intermediating a volume of credit comparable to that provided by traditional banks.[3] Figure (1) provides an approximate measure of the SB-system, based on Pozsar et al (2010), considering all the liabilities linked to "non-traditional" intermediation (like ABS, commercial paper, repos, MMMF shares).[4]

Different explanations have been given for this trend, including regulatory arbitrage or an increasing demand for riskless assets. Nonetheless, an important factor behind the fast growth of shadow banking can be clearly identified in financial innovation. In particular, the securitization process, based on combining different loans into diversified portfolios, increased the marketability of banks' assets. As a result, by broadening the array of securities available for lenders, shadow banks were able to create a new stream of outside funding. Also for this reason, they had a higher leverage capacity than traditional banks.

Even if the SB-system helped to expand credit and lower borrowing costs in the period preceding the financial crisis, it also played a crucial role in making the whole banking sector more fragile and in causing

---

[1] A survey of the different definitions and measurements of the Shadow Banking system can be found, for example, in the IMF Global Financial Stability Report of October 2014

[2] For example mortgage companies or finance companies.

[3] Private sector estimates of size vary from $10 trillion to $30 trillion (see Deloitte, 2012). A "Shadow Bank Index" developed by Deloitte put its size in the U.S.at $20 trillion in 2007. Assets intermediated by commercial banks in that period were approximately $10 trillion.

[4] The details on the data used can be found in Pozsar et al (2012), page8. Compared to Pozsar et al. I do not include GSE liabilities, since I want to focus on the part of the SB-system that did not have government sponsorship. In addition, these entities went under government conservatorship in 2008. By also adding Freddie Mac and Fannie Mae the size of the SB-system would be even larger.

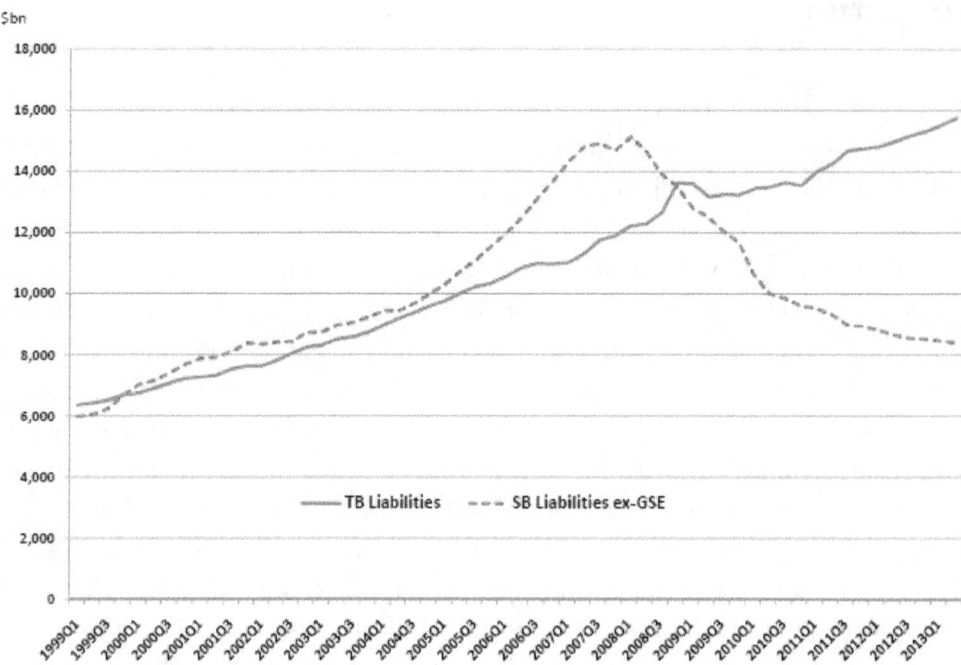

Figure 1: Liabilities of the Shadow Banking System vs liabilities of Traditional Banking System, as constructed in Pozsar et al (2012). Data from Flow of Funds Accounts of the United States as of 2013:Q2

the "Great Recession". In fact, the rise in defaults among subprime lenders triggered runs in different shadow banking markets, causing the collapse of most of these unregulated institutions and also affecting the traditional banking system.[5] It seems therefore crucial to understand the linkages between these relatively new financial structures and the real economy.

In this paper, I will model how the introduction of an additional banking sector, with a higher level of "financial sophistication", can make the economy more unstable, despite increasing credit availability; and how the interaction with the traditional banking system can create patterns similar to the ones observed in the financial crisis. The novel contribution of this work is that it captures relevant features of the Great Recession by combining shadow banks, endogenous loan quality, and bank runs in a macroeconomic model.

In particular, I consider financial intermediaries that are able to originate risky projects and screen their expected quality by exerting costly effort. However, asymmetric information, on the characteristics of the loans that banks fund, limit the amount that they can raise from outside investors. This agency problem affects differently the two types of intermediaries that I model in this paper: traditional banks (TB) and shadow banks (SB). The former are able to invest only in the projects undertaken in a single geographical location, that I call "island", whose ex-post idiosyncratic performance is only observable by the originating bank. This implies a constraint on external funds linked to the worst possible idiosyncratic realization of the assets of TBs.

On the other hand, intermediaries involved in shadow banking are assumed to have a higher level of financial innovation, and are thus able to invest in a pool of loans originated from different borrowers, improving on the ex-post observability of project outcomes. As a consequence, they can partially diversify

---

[5]See Covitz et al. (2013) for runs on ABCP programs or Gorton and Metrick (2010) for runs on repos.

the idiosyncratic risk and pledge a larger share of the return on their projects to outside lenders, by writing contracts contingent on the realization of their pool of assets. In this way, shadow banks endogenously achieve a higher leverage than traditional banks, so that the presence of the SB-system helps to expand credit and to increase investments and output.

The financial sophistication of shadow banks, however, can be costly for the aggregate economy because of the higher fragility of the financial sector. In this model such instability comes from three sources: higher leverage, lower quality of loans, and the possibility of bank runs.

First of all, the higher aggregate leverage of the banking system will amplify negative exogenous shocks, through a mechanism similar to the financial accelerator of Bernanke, Gertler and Gilchrist (1999) and Gertler and Karadi (2011).

In addition, a novelty of this model is the interaction between asset quality and leverage, as a specific feature of shadow banking: because the higher leverage is obtained by promising a higher payment to investors in case projects are successful, shadow banks have a lower incentive to screen projects, and will originate riskier loans. We can think of this as a stylized representation of the parallel boom of shadow banking and subprime lending.

The moral hazard problem that links off-balance-sheet finance and bank risk-taking represents one important aspect of securitization, as shown in Pennacchi (1988) and Fender and Mitchell (2009). In addition to being theoretically significant, this characterization of shadow banking has received wide empirical support in recent years. For example, Keys et al. (2010) find that securitized loans experienced higher default rates than similar mortgages that were instead retained by the bank. Drucker and Puri (2009) show that financial intermediaries usually sell riskier loans and provide covenants in order to reduce the problems arising from information asymmetry. Sufi (2007) shows that when borrowing firms require more intense due diligence, lenders retain a larger fraction of syndicated loans.

In this paper, I present a novel mechanism that shows the implications of this agency problem for the cyclicality of bank asset quality. During recessions, as the value of shadow bank net worth declines, so does their "skin in the game". As a result, the quality of the projects that the SB-system can credibly intermediate will endogenously deteriorate even further, causing a slower recovery of this financial sector. On the other hand, such a mechanism will be absent for traditional banks, since their funding capacity does not depend on their screening effort.

The evolution of asset quality will also translate in endogenous volatility in the cross-sectional equity returns of financial intermediaries. In fact, during a crisis the volatility in the returns of financial intermediaries, and in particular of shadow banks, will rise considerably, a type of countercyclicality that has received great attention recently.[6]

Another important source of macroeconomic instability that a setup with two types of financial intermediaries allows me to consider is the eventuality of a run on shadow banks. In particular, because of their high leverage and the type of securities they issue, shadow banks will be exposed to bank runs. On the other hand, the low leverage and the incentive constraint on their liabilities rules out this possibility for traditional banks. As a result, when a run occurs, shadow banks will have to sell their assets to traditional banks in order to repay creditors, and this fire sale, because of the limited leverage capacity of the TB-system, will depress asset prices and negatively affect investment. If prices drop enough, the run becomes self-fulfilling and most of the shadow banks are liquidated, causing a prolonged recession and a slow recovery of the financial system.

---

[6] See, for example, Christiano, Motto, and Rostagno (2014); Ferreira (2014); Christiano and Ikeda (2014).

A series of run episodes were in fact at the heart of the collapse of the shadow banking system.For example, Covitz, Liang and Suarez (2013) show how most asset backed commercial paper (ABCP) programs faced a run in 2007. As figure (2) shows, since then, the volume of outstanding ABCP, one of the main funding instruments of shadow banks, plummeted from $1.2 trillion in 2007 to about $250 billion in 2013.

Figure 2: ABCP outstanding; data from the Federal Reserve Bank of Saint Louis

The reintermediation of assets from shadow banks to traditional banks, a key element behind the negative amplification mechanisms in this model, was also an event that characterized the height of the financial turmoil. As documented by He, Khang and Krishnamurthy (2012), during the crisis hedge funds and broker-dealers reduced their holdings of securitized assets by about $800 billion, whereas traditional banks and the government increased their holdings by $550 billion and $350 billion respectively. As a result, debt issued by the traditional banking sector increased dramatically and the related leverage increased. Such reintermediation is also visible in figure (1), where we see that traditional banks liabilities jumped in 2008 and increased steadily since then.

Finally, I use this setup to analyze the implications of government policies similar to the ones that the Federal Reserve implemented in the aftermath of the crisis. With numerical experiments, I show how direct credit intermediation provided by an unconstrained government can help counter the negative feedback mechanisms described above. In particular, the presence of a central bank that helps to intermediate the assets of shadow banks in the case of a systemic run, can make the run less likely or even impossible.

The notion of shadow banking encompasses a wide universe of financial activities and economic forces, not all of which are captured in this paper. For example, I do not model any type of regulatory arbitrage motive behind shadow banking, or the sponsorship relationship between traditional banks and structured investment vehicles (SIVs) or MMMFs.[7] Also, I do not introduce any type of deposit insurance or capital

---

[7] For regulatory arbitrage see, for example, Ordonez (2013). For specific models on SIVs or MMMFs see, for example, Segura

4

requirement for traditional banks, although the friction that I consider has the similar rationale of limiting the leverage of traditional banks in order to guarantee that they are always able to repay depositors. The modeling of all these phenomena is beyond the scope of this paper, whose focus is the interaction between financial innovation, loan quality, shadow banking and macroeconomic instability.

1.1 Related Literature

This paper draws from different strands of literature related to agency problems in banking and their implications for the macroeconomy.

As regards the microfoundation for the limit on financial intermediaries leverage, my framework combines a "worst-case-scenario" constraint, similar to the one used in Carlstrom and Samolyk (1995) and Bernanke and Gertler (1987), with a moral hazard problem on monitored finance, like the one modeled by Pennacchi (1988) and Gorton and Pennacchi (1995). In particular, even if I do not model the details of securitization, the contract between shadow banks and outside investors that I use is similar to the loan sales contract described in these two papers.

An informational friction similar to the one used in this paper for shadow banks is used by Christiano and Ikeda (2014): also in their model banks can affect the probability of success of their projects by exerting costly unobservable effort. However, an important difference comes from the fact that in their framework the screening cost is not proportional to the amount of projects funded, so that no endogenous leverage constraint arises from their agency problem. In such a framework the focus of their paper is rather to study the possibility of improving welfare by introducing exogenous leverage restrictions.

Another paper in which the recovery of the financial sector is affected by an endogenous deterioration in asset quality is Bigio (2012). In Bigio (2012), this result stems from an adverse selection problem between the bank and the borrower, in which the latter provides lower quality collateral as the volume of intermediation shrinks. In addition, this mechanism is not the result of financial innovation, and affects the banking system as a whole, rather than being a specific feature of the shadow banking system.

My interpretation of shadow banking as a process to improve diversification is similar to the one used by Gennaioli et al. (2013). In their paper, banks can improve on their funding constraint by pooling different assets in order to be able to pledge the worst aggregate realization on their loans, rather than the worst idiosyncratic one. In their framework, shadow banking is driven by the demand for riskless assets by infinitely risk-averse depositors, and it becomes detrimental only when investors neglect tail risk. As mentioned in the introduction, other papers have modeled shadow banking as stemming from regulatory arbitrage, like Plantin (2012) or Ordonez (2013).

Recently many macroeconomic models with a financial sector have been developed (e.g. Gertler and Karadi (2011), Brunnermeier and Sannikov (2011), He and Krishnamurthy (2012)), but there have been only a few attempts to include shadow banks and their exposure to runs in a general-equilibrium setting. For example, Meeks et al. (2013) introduce in the framework of Gertler and Karadi (2011) a SB sector that funds itself from traditional banks, and assume that traditional banks have a weaker friction when investing in shadow bank liabilities. However, in such a setup, there is no role for loan quality and a run on the SB-system, started by outside investors, is not possible. Faia (2012) studies the effect of a secondary market for loans in a DSGE model with a moral hazard problem similar to the one I consider, but where loan quality is determined exogenously and only one type of intermediary is present.

(2014) or Parlatore (2013).

As regards the modeling of bank runs in general equilibrium, my approach is similar to the one used by Gertler and Kiyotaki (2014). An important difference is that in their paper, when a run occurs assets are directly acquired by households that incur a real cost to manage capital. It is this cost that determines the liquidation price and that makes a run possible. On the other hand, in my setup a run occurs because of the fire sale of assets from shadow banks to traditional banks with a lower leverage capacity. Other macroeconomic models of bank runs are Martin, Skeie, and Von Thadden (2012) and Angeloni and Faia (2013).

The rest of the paper is organized as follows. Section 2 describes the asymmetric information problem in the financial sector and the optimal contract for a financial intermediary operating as a traditional bank or as a shadow bank. Section 3 presents the baseline model where both traditional banks and shadow banks are present. Section 4 explains how a run on the shadow banking system is possible in this model. Section 5 shows a first set of numerical exercises with crisis experiments and run experiments. Section 6 introduces government intervention and studies its interaction with financial crises and the possibility of a run. Finally, Section 7 concludes.

2 Risky Projects and Financial Intermediaries

I begin by describing the agency problems affecting the two types of financial intermediaries present in this framework, and by solving the related optimal contracts. I then proceed to embed the financial system so characterized in a medium-scale macroeconomic model.

One of the distinguishing features of banks in this model is that they are the only type of agent able to invest in risky projects, by financing capital purchases of productive firms. In particular, I assume that there are two "regions", each with a continuum of firms located on a continuum of islands.[8] On every island, firms can invest in risky projects k_t , or "raw capital", that will be employed in a constant-return-to-scale production technology at time t+1.

Capital is risky because it can turn into $\theta_H k_t$ units of productive capital next period if the project succeeds or $\theta_L k_t$ if the project fails, with $\theta_H > \theta_L$. Projects on a specific island will be perfectly correlated, so that they either all fail or all succeed. However, I assume that the probability of success p differs across the two regions. In particular the two regions will be perfectly negatively correlated, so that every period one region will be "good", whereas the other one will be "bad". The difference between a region that turns out to be good and one that instead is bad is in the probability of success of loans p^G and p_t^B, where $p^G > p_t^B$.

$$Good \longrightarrow \begin{cases} \theta_H & \text{w.p.} & p^G \\ \theta_L & \text{w.p.} & (1-p^G) \end{cases} \qquad Bad \longrightarrow \begin{cases} \theta_H & \text{w.p.} & p_t^B \\ \theta_L & \text{w.p.} & (1-p_t^B) \end{cases}$$

Therefore, the proportion of islands with successful projects will be p^G in the good region and p_t^B in the bad one. In addition to assuming a higher probability of default in the bad region, I will also allow for iid disturbances to p_t^B in order to capture, in a stylized way, a "subprime shock" that only affects the return on lower quality loans. Define the average realization of a project, conditional on the type of region as $\bar{\theta}^j$ for $j = G, B$, where

$$\bar{\theta}^G = p^G \theta_H + (1-p^G)\theta_L \text{ and } \bar{\theta}_t^B = p_t^B \theta_H + (1-p_t^B)\theta_L \tag{1}$$

---

[8]An alternative interpretation is that of two "sectors". What is going to be important in the characterization of the setup is just the presence of a double layer of randomness in the outcome structure of projects.

It is important to stress that financial intermediaries are going to finance projects in an island in a given region at time t, without knowing whether that region will be good or bad at time $t + 1$, and whether projects in a specific island will be successful or not. However, banks can exert effort e_t in order to increase the probability $\pi_t(e_t)$ of selecting a loan in a region that will be good next period. For simplicity I assume that this probability is linear in effort, according to $\pi_t = e_t$, so that we can refer to π_t also as screening level. Imporantly, effort is costly, since it entails a non-percuniary convex cost $c(e_t) = c(\pi_t)$, per unit of capital intermediated. In particular I assume $c(\pi_t) = \frac{\tau}{2}\left(\pi_t^2 + \iota\pi_t\right)$ and I allow for ι to be negative, meaning that there could be some benefits from screening.[9] However I consider calibrations where $c'(\pi_t) > 0$ meaning that it is costly for financial intermediaries to increase their screening effort.

We can define the expected quality of a project with screening intensity π_t as

$$E_t\left[\Theta_{t+1}(\pi_t)\right] = E_t\left[\pi_t\bar{\theta}^G + (1 - \pi_t)\bar{\theta}_{t+1}^B\right] \tag{2}$$

Importantly, banks cannot perfectly diversify across all islands. This limit to diversification implies that the assets intermediated by each bank are risky and, as it will be clear below, it allows asymmetric information on bank portfolios to create a relevant agency problem.

In addition, as I mentioned in the introduction, I consider two types of intermediaries, traditional banks and shadow banks, differing in the ability to diversify across islands. In particular I assume that TBs are only able to invest in projects in one single island, that next period will deliver θ_H units of productive capital in case of success and θ_L in case of failure. On the other hand, SBs are able to invest in a "pool" of loans located in the same region. As a result, the outcome of the shadow bank's portfolio will be either $\bar{\theta}^G$ if the region is good or $\bar{\theta}_{t+1}^B$ if it is bad.

This framework is equivalent to one in which shadow banks purchase loans originated by a set of traditional banks located in the same region.[10] As long as these loans are purchased at their market value, implying zero profits for the TB on these projects, the structure of the model would be identical. What I am trying to model in this way, is the practice of pooling mortgages that was behind the rapid development of securitization and the shadow banking system.

It needs to be noticed that even if SBs are more diversified than TBs, they will still be exposed to some idiosyncratic risk. As a supporting piece of evidence for this assumption, we can think of the fact that securitized products mainly comprised loans belonging to a single asset class (credit-cards, mortages student loans etc.), hence being far from perfect diversification.

The different level of diversification will play an important role in determining the funding constraints for the two types of financial intermediaries because of two layers of information asymmetries:

1. **Unobservable Outcome** (UO):

    - the default realization of loans (θ_L, θ_H), on a given island, is only observable by the originating bank

    - the type-realization of a specific region (good or bad) is public information.

2. **Unobservable Effort** (UE): the screening level of the loans that a bank funds (π_t^j for $j = tb, sb$) is private information

---

[9]The theoretical results of the paper hold for a generic quadratic cost function $c(\pi_t) = \frac{\tau}{2}\left(\pi_t^2 + \iota\pi_t + \varepsilon\right)$, but the specific form used has the advantage of providing a closed form solution for the optimal π_t chosen by each type of intermediary.

[10]With this interpretation the π_t chosen by shadow banks would represent the probability of purchasing projects from traditional banks located in a good region.

As a consequence of the different diversification abilities of the two intermediaries, the first friction (UO) will characterize the contracting problem between households and TBs whereas the second one (UE) will be at the core of the funding constraint for the SB system.[11]

The crucial distinction between the two types of contracts will depend on the observability of the ex-post realization of the loan portfolio held by each intermediary. In fact, because of the UO-friction, TBs can credibly commit only to a payment linked to the worst possible realization of their projects. On the other hand, since the outcome of their pool of loans is verifiable, SBs will be able to write a contract contingent on the idiosyncratic realization of their assets. We can think of this framework as capturing the idea that, by combining several loans, shadow banks created securities that were easier to evaluate for a rating agency and hence easier to pledge to external investors.[12]

In particular I will show that traditional banks will have a smaller endogenous leverage than shadow banks. In addition, unlike the case for SB, the funding capacity of traditional banks will not depend on the expected quality of the loans they hold.

The idea behind this setup is that of a SB system that, because of financial products that exploit risk diversification, is able to increase the marketability of bank loans and to improve on the capital constraints affecting the traditional banking system, hence intermediating funds with a lower level of net worth.

Given this characterization of the financial system, I will first derive the optimal contract for financial intermediaries in a first-best scenario when no asymmetric information is present and both the outcome and the riskiness of a project are observable. This will serve as a benchmark to identify the inefficiencies arising from the agency problems of the two types of banks.

I will then derive the optimal contract for a traditional bank and the one for a shadow bank. In the baseline model, I will consider an economy where both types of intermediaries are present, as it was the case for the U.S. economy in the years preceding the financial crisis. The focus of this model is not to provide a specific economic mechanism to explain the growth of the shadow banking system, but rather to take its existence, size and agency problems as given, in order to study its macroeconomic effects.

2.1 The Optimal Contract in the Frictionless Economy

In this subsection I assume that there is no asymmetric information problem affecting the banking sector. I will refer to this scenario as the "Frictionless Economy" or "First-Best Economy".

Let Q_t be the price of a unit of capital at time t, and R_{t+1}^k the return per unit of effective capital at time $t+1$. As I will explain in more detail below, I assume that firms are competitive and that there is no agency problem between banks and entrepreneurs. Therefore, a bank will finance the total capital expenditures $k_t Q_t$ faced by each firm and will receive the risky return per dollar invested, $\theta^j R_{t+1}^k$, for $j = H, L$, depending on whether the specific project is successful or not.

At the beginning of time t, a bank enters the economy with an initial net worth n_t and has to decide the amount of projects to finance k_t and the screening intensity π_t. The required amount of external funding

---

[11] As an additional technical condition, I assume that at the moment of signing the contract with a bank (CB or SB), the individual household does not observe the distribution of financial intermediaries across the islands. Equivalently we can think that bank receives funds before having selected the specific island(s) where to invest.This simply rules out that investors are able to perfectly foresee which sector is good by inferring the monitoring level selected by intermediaries.

[12] It has to be noted that here we are referring to ex-post observability. The ex-ante riskiness of loans, depending on π, will still be unobservable also for shadow banks and will be behind the agency problem that affects shadow banking funding.

provided by households will hence have to be

$$s_t = Q_t k_t - n_t$$

In this instance, I assume that the bank has access to the most efficient diversification technology available in the economy, that is the one used by shadow banks, which allows the financial intermediary to invest in a pool of projects in a specific region. As a result, the optimal contract will specify a pair of payments to outside lenders per unit of capital , $b_{t+1}^{G,fb}$ and $b_{t+1}^{B,fb}$, contingent on whether the pool of loans is good or bad. In particular, these payments will have to satisfy the following participation constraint for the household

$$Q_t k_t - n_t \leq E_t \Lambda_{t,t+1} \left[\pi_t^{fb} b_{t+1}^{G,fb} + (1 - \pi_t^{fb}) b_{t+1}^{B,fb} \right] Q_t k_t \tag{3}$$

where $\Lambda_{t,t+1}$ represents the household stochastic discount factor, and π_t^{fb} is the screening level chosen in the frictionless case.

In addition, I assume limited liability for the financial intermediary, so that for every realization of projects outcome the payment to households cannot be larger than the assets available to the bank, that is

$$b_{t+1}^{G,fb} \leq \bar{\theta}^G R_{t+1}^k \tag{4}$$

$$b_{t+1}^{B,fb} \leq \bar{\theta}_{t+1}^B R_{t+1}^k \tag{5}$$

As mentioned in the introduction, financial intermediaries are able to increase the probability of selecting a good project, π_t, by facing a non-pecuniary cost, $c(\pi_t)$, proportional to the value of the loans financed. In particular, I assume $c(\pi_t) = \frac{\tau_t}{2} \left(\pi_t^2 + \iota \pi \right)$,

To solve the optimal contract we have to maximize the following bank objective:

$$\max_{k_t, \pi_t, b_{t+1}^g, b_{t+1}^h} Q_t k_t \left\{ E_t \Lambda_{t,t+1} \left[\pi_t^{fb} \left(\bar{\theta}^G R_{t+1}^k - b_{t+1}^{G,fb} \right) + (1 - \pi_t^{fb}) \left(\bar{\theta}^B R_{t+1}^k - b_{t+1}^{B,fb} \right) \right] - c \left(\pi_t^{fb} \right) \right\}$$

subject to (3), (4) and (5).

The objective function of the bank includes the expected return from the pool of projects, net of the payments to outside creditors and the screening costs. In particular, given that the bank is owned by the representative household, as will be explained in the next section, it discounts future profits with the same discount factor.

In the appendix, it is shown that the first order conditions of this problem imply the following

$$c' \left(\pi_t^{fb} \right) = E_t \Lambda_{t,t+1} \bar{\Delta}_{t+1} R_{t+1}^k \tag{6}$$

$$E_t \Lambda_{t,t+1} \left\{ \left[\pi_t^{fb} \bar{\theta}^G + \left(1 - \pi_t^{fb} \right) \bar{\theta}_{t+1}^B \right] R_{t+1}^k - R_{t+1} \right\} - c \left(\pi_t^{fb} \right) = 0 \tag{7}$$

where $\bar{\Delta}_{t+1} = \left(\bar{\theta}^G - \bar{\theta}_{t+1}^B \right)$ and I used $E_t \Lambda_{t,t+1} R_{t+1} = 1$.

Equation (6) determines how the screening effort is optimally chosen in the frictionless scenario. It equates the marginal cost of screening to the social marginal benefit, which is given by the extra return generated by good projects with respect to bad ones. In addition, equation (7) equalizes the expected return on capital, net of the screening cost, to the risk-free rate. This is a standard no-arbitrage condition for a model with perfect capital markets.

Combining these two equations we can determine the risk-adjusted return to capital $E_t\Lambda_{t,t+1}R_{t+1}^k$, and consequently the level of capital in the economy. In this frictionless scenario, if we focus on first order effects, this quantity will generally not move over time.[13] On the other hand, as will become clear in the following sections, when there is a binding agency problem equation (7) will not hold with equality, implying a positive premium on the adjusted return to capital, a distinguishing feature of macroeconomic models with financial frictions. In addition, the movements in this premium will be important for the cyclicality of investments and , a unique feature of this model, asset quality.

In the first best contract, $b_{t+1}^{G,fb}$ and $b_{t+1}^{B,fb}$ are not uniquely determined; any pair of payments satisfying (3), (4) and (5) would be admissible. Finally, it is important to notice that in this case bank net worth does not play a role in determining aggregate demand for capital, and that the optimal contract does not constrain the financial leverage $\phi_t = Q_t k_t/n_t$.

2.2 The Optimal Contract for Traditional Banks

Let us now consider the optimal contract for a financial intermediary operating with the traditional banking technology. There is a continuum of traditional banks, each providing funds to non-financial firms located in one single island. Each traditional bank finances the investment in its projects, $Q_t k_t^{tb}$, by using its own net worth, n_t^{tb}, and by issuing liabilities s_t^{tb}.

The balance sheet of a traditional bank will then be

$$Q_t k_t^{tb} = n_t^{tb} + s_t^{tb} \tag{8}$$

Because of the (UO) friction described above, traditional banks will be limited in the amount they can pledge to repay depositors. In particular, similarly to Townsend (1979), the payment to lenders cannot be contingent on the idiosyncratic realization of the loans, since this is not observable, so that $b_{t+1}^{G,tb} = b_{t+1}^{B,tb} = b_{t+1}^{tb}$. In addition, for the amount that traditional banks commit to repay to be incentive-compatible, this will have to satisfy the following incentive constraint

$$b_{t+1}^{tb} \leq \theta_L R_{t+1}^k \tag{9}$$

This constraint comes from the fact that households cannot observe whether the loans held by the traditional bank have defaulted or not, hence, the only payment that can be enforced is linked to the worst possible idiosyncratic realization, since in this case the bank would not have incentives to misreport. Importantly, this "worst-case-scenario constraint" also guarantees that the traditional bank will always be able to repay its creditors, which is why we can also refer to (9) as a "solvency constraint". A similar type of funding constraint can be found in other papers such as Bernanke and Gertler (1987) and Carlstrom and Samolyk (1995). In addition, also Gennaioli et al. (2012) use a similar limit on bank deposits, but in their case it is motivated by extreme risk-aversion among depositors rather than by asymmetric information.

Notice that in this setup, if (9) binds, the return on s_t^{tb} will be devoid of idiosyncratic risk but will be exposed to aggregate risk. In this sense, we can think of s_t^{tb} as including both deposits and other types of non-risk-free securities, like preferred equity.[14] The important aspect is that since the payment is going to

---

[13]This is true unless there is a shock to $\bar{\theta}_{t+1}^B$

[14]In particular, it can be shown that the payment implied by the optimal contract can be implemented as a combination of risk-free debt, equity, and a bonus to bankers in case the project is successful.

be contingent on the aggregate price Q_t, traditional banks will always be able to repay their creditors.[15] In addition, this result will also imply that they will not be exposed to bank runs.

The implied objective for the traditional bank is therefore

$$E_t Q_t k_t^{tb} \{ \Lambda_{t,t+1} \left[\left(\pi_t^{tb} \bar{\theta}^G + \left(1 - \pi_t^{tb} \right) \bar{\theta}_{t+1}^B \right) R_{t+1}^k - b_{t+1}^{tb} \right] - c(\pi_t^{tb}) \}$$

Finally, when solving for the optimal contract we also have to take into account the participation constraint (PC) that guarantees that creditors receive an appropriate return on their lending activity

$$s_t^{tb} \leq E_t \Lambda_{t,t+1} b_{t+1}^{tb} Q_t k_t^{tb} \tag{10}$$

This is going to be the same relationship implied by households first order condition for the choice of traditional banks securities.

Given these assumptions, the one period contract between the TB and households will have to solve

$$\max_{k_t^{tb}, \pi_t^{tb}, s_t^{tb}, b_{t+1}^{tb}} E_t Q_t k_t^{tb} \{ \Lambda_{t,t+1} \left[\Theta_{t+1}(\pi_t^{tb}) R_{t+1}^k - b_{t+1}^{tb} \right] - c(\pi_t^{tb}) \}$$

$$\text{s.t } b_{t+1}^{tb} \leq \theta_L R_{t+1}^k \quad \text{(IC)}$$

$$\left(Q_t k_t^{tb} - n_t^{tb} \right) \leq E_t \beta \Lambda_{t,t+1} b_{t+1}^{tb} Q_t k_t^{tb} \quad \text{(PC)}$$

It can be shown that when the incentive constraint binds [16], then the following will be true

$$E_t \Lambda_{t,t+1} \left[\Theta_{t+1}(\pi_t^{tb}) R_{t+1}^k - R_{t+1} \right] - c(\pi_t^{tb}) > 0$$

This inequality shows the presence of a wedge between the discounted return on borrowers assets and the cost of funds (R_{t+1}), two values that were equal in the first best scenario. This is a classic result in models with financial frictions, but in this framework it is enriched by the endogenous choice of asset quality.

The incentive constraint will also limit the amount of assets that traditional banks can intermediate by implying a constraint on their leverage, $\phi_t^{tb} = \frac{Q_t k_t^{tb}}{n_t^{tb}}$, given by

$$\phi_t^{tb} \leq \frac{1}{\left[1 - \theta_L E_t \Lambda_{t,t+1} R_{t+1}^k \right]} \tag{11}$$

We can give an intuitive interpretation to this relationship. First of all, the leverage capacity is increasing in the expected aggregate return to capital $E_t \Lambda_{t,t+1} R_{t+1}^k$, since it increases the amount that can be credibly promised to external investors. For the same reason, leverage will be higher the higher θ_L, the recovery rate on defaulted projects. It is also important to notice that the debt capacity of traditional banks is not directly linked to the riskiness of their loans, π_t^{tb}. This is a consequence of the fact that traditional banks can only pledge the worst possible realization, independently from the outcome of their projects.

As a result, the first order condition on the screening level will determine π_t^{tb} in a similar fashion to what

---

[15]It would be possible to slightly modify the assumptions of the agency problem in order to have the TB issuing risk-free debt as well. For example one could assume that if the project fails it delivers a predetermined amount of goods $\theta_L k_t$. However such feature would not add to the dynamics of the model and it would make the characterization of the contract less intuitive. In addition, a framework in which also TB issue risk-free securities would amplify all the mechanisms in this paper because of a higher financial accelerator in the TB sector.

[16]See appendix for a detailed solution of the contract.

occurred in the frictionless scenario, that is according to

$$c'(\pi_t^{tb}) = E_t \Lambda_{t,t+1} \bar{\Delta}_{t+1} R_{t+1}^k \tag{12}$$

The intuition for this result is the following: since the payment to households does not depend on whether the loan will be in a good or bad region, the traditional bank will retain all the exposure to the idiosyncratic risk and hence it will equalize the marginal cost of monitoring to the expected social marginal benefit, given by the extra expected return that a good project delivers. In terms of the dynamics of traditional bank monitoring, this equation will imply countercyclical movements in the quality of their loans, since in recessions the marginal value of monitoring will be higher, due to a larger discounted expected return on capital.

If we use the specific functional form for the cost function , from (12) we can directly obtain the optimal level of π_t^{tb} set by the traditional bank as

$$\pi_t^{tb} = \frac{E_t \Lambda_{t,t+1} \bar{\Delta}_{t+1} R_{t+1}^k}{\tau_t} - \frac{\tau_t}{2} \iota \tag{13}$$

which also shows how π_t^{tb} is decreasing in the parameter affecting the marginal cost of screening, given by τ_t.

At this point, we can define the return that households obtain after lending to traditional banks as

$$R_t^{tb} = \theta_L R_t^k \frac{\phi_{t-1}^{tb}}{\phi_{t-1}^{tb} - 1} \tag{14}$$

From the equations above, we notice how both the leverage ratio and the screening intensity of traditional banks only depend on aggregate quantities, allowing for an easy aggregation. In addition, equation (14) implies that R_t^{tb} only depends on aggregate variables.

2.3   The Optimal Contract for Shadow Banks

Shadow banks have access to the same screening technology of traditional banks. However, they can use a special diversification technology that allows them to "pool" projects within a single region. As described above, the type-realization of a region, that is whether it is good or bad, is publicly observable, enabling shadow banks to overcome the UO-friction that affects the relationship between households and traditional banks. However, since the diversification is not complete, shadow banks will still be exposed to some idiosyncratic risk. Because of this, it will be the unobservability of the monitoring effort chosen, π_t^{sb}, coming from the UE-friction, that will constrain the amount of funds that shadow banks can raise.

The shadow bank will fund its capital, k_t^{sb}, by using its net worth and by issuing securities, s_t^{sb}. Its balance sheet will then be

$$Q_t k_t^{sb} = n_t^{sb} + s_t^{sb} \tag{15}$$

Unlike the case for traditional banks, the contract between shadow banks and outside investors will specify payments to the households, per dollar of loan, that are contingent on the realized type of the loan pool, that is b_{t+1}^j for $j = G, B$. Again, because of limited liability, we require

$$b_{t+1}^{j,sb} \le \bar{\theta}_{t+1}^j R_{t+1}^k \text{ for } j = G, B \tag{16}$$

12

Note that this setup has some similarities to the pooling and tranching that was behind securitization, because we could interpret this contract as the shadow bank selling a contingent claim to the outcome of its pool of loans in return for an amount s_t^{sb}, similarly to the notion of "loan sale" presented in Pennacchi (1988).

The expected return for the shadow bank, including the non-pecuniary monitoring costs, will be given by

$$Q_t k_t \left\{ E_t \Lambda_{t,t+1} \left[\pi_t^{sb} \left(\bar{\theta}^G R_{t+1}^k - b_{t+1}^{G,sb} \right) + (1 - \pi_t^{sb}) \left(\bar{\theta}^B R_{t+1}^k - b_{t+1}^{B,sb} \right) \right] - c \left(\pi_t^{sb} \right) \right\} \tag{17}$$

Importantly, because of the UE-friction, the contract for SBs will be characterized by a moral hazard problem with hidden action. In particular, this is due to the fact that the payment to investors depends on the quality of the loans originated by the shadow bank, π_t^{sb}, which is unobservable by outsiders.

Therefore, an incentive constraint (IC), that guarantees that the shadow bank will select a given screening level, will be required:

$$\pi_t^{sb} = \arg\max_{\pi_t^{sb}} \left\{ E_t \Lambda_{t,t+1} \left[\pi_t^{sb} \left(\bar{\theta}^G R_{t+1}^k - b_{t+1}^{G,sb} \right) + (1 - \pi_t^{sb}) \left(\bar{\theta}^B R_{t+1}^k - b_{t+1}^{B,sb} \right) \right] - c \left(\pi_t^{sb} \right) \right\} \tag{18}$$

In addition, because the simple way in which banks can affect the loans return distribution satisfies the "convexity-of-distribution-function" condition described in Hart and Holmstrom (1986), we can write the (IC) in a more tractable way, by using the first order conditions of (18), that is

$$c' \left(\pi_t^{sb} \right) \leq E_t \Lambda_{t,t+1} \left[\bar{\Delta}_{t+1} R_{t+1}^k - \left(b_{t+1}^{G,sb} - b_{t+1}^{B,sb} \right) \right] \tag{19}$$

It has to be noted that such a constraint does not bind in the problem of TBs, since the payment that they promise to outsiders does not depend on the idiosyncratic realization of their projects.

Finally, we have to consider the participation constraint for lenders, which guarantees that the household obtains an expected return equal to the opportunity cost of its funds. As in Bernanke, Gertler, and Gilchrist (1999), I assume that the shadow banker is willing to bear all the aggregate risk, guaranteeing a payment to the lender that is equal to the risk-free rate in expectation.[17] As a result the participation constraint will imply restrictions on $b_{t+1}^{G,sb}, b_{t+1}^{B,sb}$ contingent on the realization of the aggregate shock, according to

$$R_{t+1} s_t^{sb} \leq \left[\pi_t^{sb} b_{t+1}^{G,sb} + (1 - \pi_t^{sb}) b_{t+1}^{B,sb} \right] Q_t k_t^{sb} \tag{20}$$

If we focus on a parametrization that allows for a value of $b_{t+1}^{G,sb}, b_{t+1}^{B,sb}$ satisfying (20) and (16) to exist for any aggregate state,[18] then the household can diversify the residual idiosyncratic risk by investing in "mutual funds" that lend money to several shadow banks, and promise a rate of return equal to the risk-free rate.[19] Hence, in this framework we can think of the security s_t^{sb}, as ABCP or shares of a MMMF.

In this setup, shadow banks are hence retaining all the exposure to fluctuations in asset prices and default rates, and they issue to the mutual fund a senior claim on the return from their loans. Such a configuration is in line with the idea that even with the development of the "originate-to-distribute" model, which marked

---

[17] This assumption is mainly made to capture the fact that most of the liabilities issued by the shadow banks, like ABCP, were short-term non-contingent debt, that exposed the system to runs.

[18] As I will explain in Section 5, such condition will not hold in the case of a run on shadow banks. However, since the run is an unanticipated event it does not enter the optimal contract.

[19] It is relevant to notice that, because of the UO-friction, diversification across commercial banks does not alter the structure of the contract, and its payments. This depends on the fact that households are only able to require the same individual payment of $\theta_L R_t^k$ from all the CB located on different islands.

the growth of the shadow banking system, most of the risk remained inside the financial sector, as noted, among others, by Acharya, Schnabl and Suarez. (2013). In addition, this will imply that when there is a low realization of R_{t+1}^k, $b_{t+1}^{G,sb}$ will have to rise, so that the banks with a good pool of loans will have to pay a higher amount to households, diminishing their net worth. Such mechanism will play an important role in all the quantitative experiments, including the run.

Importantly, all these considerations are valid only in the "no-run equilibrium". In fact, as I will explain later in the paper, the economy will admit an alternative "run-equilibrium", in which the payment implied by the liquidation price and (20) would be such that $b_{t+1}^G > \bar{\theta}_{t+1}^G R_{t+1}^k$, thereby violating limited liability. However, if we consider only unanticipated runs, this characterization for the optimal contract remains valid in the baseline economy.

The problem of the shadow bank can therefore be written as

$$\max_{k_t^{sb},\pi_t^{sb},b_{t+1}^g,b_{t+1}^b} Q_t k_t^{sb} \left\{ E_t \Lambda_{t,t+1} \left[\pi_t^{sb} \left(\bar{\theta}^G R_{t+1}^k - b_{t+1}^{G,sb} \right) + (1 - \pi_t^{sb}) \left(\bar{\theta}^B R_{t+1}^k - b_{t+1}^{B,sb} \right) \right] - c \left(\pi_t^{sb} \right) \right\}$$

$$\text{s.t.} \quad R_{t+1} \left(Q_t k_t^{sb} - n_t^{sb} \right) \leq \left[\pi_t^{sb} b_{t+1}^{G,sb} + (1 - \pi_t^{sb}) b_{t+1}^{B,sb} \right] Q_t k_t^{sb} \quad \text{(PC)}$$

$$c' \left(\pi_t^{sb} \right) \leq E_t \Lambda_{t,t+1} \left[\bar{\Delta}_{t+1} R_{t+1}^k - \left(b_{t+1}^{G,sb} - b_{t+1}^{B,sb} \right) \right] \quad \text{(IC)}$$

$$b_{t+1}^{G,sb} \leq \bar{\theta}^G R_{t+1}^k \quad \text{(LL}^G\text{)}$$

$$b_{t+1}^{B,sb} \leq \bar{\theta}^B R_{t+1}^k \quad \text{(LL}^B\text{)}$$

where the last two equations represent limited liability constraints for each idiosyncratic realization.

The first result that can be proved is that if the (IC) binds then it will be optimal to pay the bank only in case the pool belongs to a good region, so that $b_{t+1}^{B,sb} = \bar{\theta}_{t+1}^B R_{t+1}^k$.[20] This result follows from the finding (see Hart and Holstrom (1986)) that, in order to provide incentives to monitor, it is optimal to give the worst possible punishment to the agent when the bad realization occurs. Therefore, the contract for the shadow bank will imply that if the pool of loans reveals to be a bad one, the whole return will be given to creditors and the shadow bank will default, resembling a risky debt contract.[21] As a result, we can rewrite the (IC) as

$$c' \left(\pi_t^{sb} \right) \leq E_t \Lambda_{t,t+1} \left[\bar{\theta}^G R_{t+1}^k - b_{t+1}^{G,sb} \right]$$

In addition, if the (IC) is binding then it can be shown that the following inequalities must be true

$$E_t \Lambda_{t,t+1} \left\{ \left[\pi_t^{sb} \bar{\theta}^G + (1 - \pi_t^{sb}) \bar{\theta}_{t+1}^B \right] R_{t+1}^k - R_{t+1} \right\} - c \left(\pi_t^{sb} \right) > 0 \tag{21}$$

$$c'(\pi_t^{sb}) < E_t \Lambda_{t,t+1} \bar{\Delta}_{t+1} R_{t+1}^k \tag{22}$$

The first inequality is analogous to the one obtained in the problem for the traditional bank: also in this case the incentive constraint implies that the discounted return on bank assets is larger than the cost of funds.

In addition, the second inequality implies that, given the same $E_t \Lambda_{t,t+1} \bar{\Delta}_{t+1} R_{t+1}^k$, the quality of loans originated by shadow banks will be lower than the one of traditional banks.[22] This result comes from the

---

[20]Details for the solution of the optimal contract can be found in the appendix.

[21]A similar result is derived in Pennacchi (1988), where the loan's return density is a continuous function with bounded support.

[22]This will be the case in the baseline model, where both TB and SB operate and $E_t \Lambda_{t,t+1} \bar{\Delta}_{t+1} R_{t+1}^k$ only depends on

fact that, unlike the traditional bank, the shadow bank does not retain all the idiosyncratic risk coming from the choice of π_t^{sb}. By being able to pledge a larger portion of the return on its loans, the shadow bank does not internalize all the expected benefits from monitoring, that is $E_t\Lambda_{t,t+1}\bar{\Delta}_{t+1}R_{t+1}^k$. As a result it will have lower incentives to screen its projects.

Furthermore, from the PC we obtain that

$$b_{t+1}^{G,sb} = \frac{1}{\pi_t^{sb}}\left[R_{t+1}\frac{(\phi_t-1)}{\phi_t} - (1-\pi_t^{sb})\bar{\theta}^b R_{t+1}^k\right] \tag{23}$$

and by substituting the implied value of $b_{t+1}^{G,sb}$ in (19) we obtain that the (IC) imposes the following leverage constraint for shadow banks

$$\phi_t^{sb} \leq \frac{1}{\left\{\pi_t^{sb}c'(\pi_t^{sb}) - \left[E_t\Lambda_{t,t+1}\Theta_{t+1}\left(\pi_t^{sb}\right)R_{t+1}^k - 1\right]\right\}} \tag{24}$$

where

$$\phi_t^{sb} = \frac{Q_t k_t^{sb}}{n_t^{sb}}$$

In this case ϕ_t^{sb} is increasing in the total expected return on the pool of loans, whereas it is decreasing in the expected payment due to the bank $\pi_t^{sb}\left[\bar{\theta}^G R_{t+1}^k - b_{t+1}^{G,sb}\right] = \pi_t^{sb}c'\left(\pi_t^{sb}\right)$. In particular, a very important consequence of (24) is that it implies a negative relationship between screening effort and leverage for the shadow banks. In fact, because of the moral hazard problem related to the unobservability of π_t^{sb}, in order for the shadow bank to have incentives to exert a higher effort, it will need to have more "skin in the game" to internalize the benefits of a larger π_t^{sb}. This is accomplished by requiring that the bank covers a larger share of the investment with its own net worth, implying a lower leverage. In fact, as equation (23) suggests, a lower leverage implies a higher payment to the bank in case of success, consequently increasing its incentive to screen projects, as shown in the (IC).

Equation (24) represents an important difference from the model of Christiano and Ikeda (2014). Since in their framework the screening effort is not proportional to the amount of capital financed by the financial intermediary, the unobservability of bank effort does not imply any limit to the amount of debt that the bank can raise. This comes from the fact that the screening cost is not increasing with the amount of loans originated. As a result, in the unobservable effort scenario of Christiano and Ikeda (2014) equation (21) holds with equality and aggregate net worth does not directly affect investments. On the other hand, as it will be clear in subsequent sections, the interaction between loan quality, leverage constraints and net worth will play a crucial role in determining the aggregate dynamics of the shadow banking system and of the whole economy.

In addition, it can be shown that

$$\phi_t^{sb} > \phi_t^{tb} \tag{25}$$

This can be easily seen by using (22) when comparing (24) with (11). The intuition is that, when the IC binds, the pledgeable income per unit of capital of shadow banks, $E_t\Lambda_{t,t+1}\left[\Theta_{t+1}\left(\pi_t^{sb}\right)R_{t+1}^k\right] - \pi_t^{sb}c'\left(\pi_t^{sb}\right)$ will be larger than the one of traditional banks, $\theta^L E_t\Lambda_{t,t+1}R_{t+1}^k$. As a result, shadow banks need a lower net worth to fund the same quantity of loans.

It has to be noted that, even if we assumed that also the type realization of a region was unobservable,

---

aggregate quantities.

15

shadow banks would still have a higher leverage. This comes from the fact that, because of diversification, the worst possible outcome for a pool of projects financed by a shadow bank would be $\bar{\theta}_{t+1}^{B}$, which is greater or equal than θ^L. Therefore, even if they had to face the same type of contract used by traditional banks, shadow banks would still be able to promise a larger expected return to investors, thus obtaining a higher leverage. From this perspective, the relationship between shadow banking and diversification is similar to the one presented in Gennaioli et al. (2012), where by diversifying among themselves banks are able to offer a payment linked to the aggregate "worst case scenario" rather than to the idiosyncratic one. In addition to this mechanism, my model also introduces endogenous screening performed by intermediaries and captures a link between shadow banking and laxer lending standards, which will play an important role in the crisis experiments shown in the next section.

The inverse relationship between leverage and screening will be crucial to determine the cyclicality of the asset quality of shadow banks. In particular, π_t^{sb} will be determined by the following equation

$$\left[E\Lambda_{t,t+1}\bar{\Delta}R_{t+1}^k - c'\left(\pi_t^{sb}\right)\right]\left\{\pi_t^{sb}c'\left(\pi_t^{sb}\right) - c\left(\pi_t^{sb}\right)\right\} = \left\{E_t\Lambda_{t,t+1}\left[\Theta\left(\pi_t^{sb}\right)R_{t+1}^k - R_{t+1}\right] - c\left(\pi_t^{sb}\right)\right\}\left[\pi_t^{sb}c''\left(\pi_t^{sb}\right)\right] \tag{26}$$

implying

$$\pi_t^{sb} = \varphi(E_t\Lambda_{t,t+1}R_{t+1}^k) \quad \text{where} \quad \frac{\partial\varphi}{\partial E_t\Lambda_{t,t+1}R_{t+1}^k} < 0 \tag{27}$$

The quantity $E_t\Lambda_{t,t+1}R_{t+1}^k$ can be interpreted as the "external finance premium" defined by Bernanke, Gertler, and Gilchrist (1999). As equation (21) shows, an increase in the discounted return to capital is associated with a tightening of the incentive constraint, so that we can interpret equation (27) as a negative relationship between the quality of shadow banks loans and the severity of their agency problem. In fact, during a crisis the net worth of financial intermediaries is eroded, causing a decrease in capital demand, a consequent drop in prices and an increase in leverage together with $E_t\Lambda_{t,t+1}R_{t+1}^k$. As a result of the higher leverage, the shadow bank will have a lower level of "skin in the game" in the projects that it originates, and consequently it will be able to credibly commit to a lower level of π_t^{sb}. The relationship in (27) will play an important role in the model dynamics. In fact, it will imply that when a negative shock hits the economy the quality of the loans intermediated by shadow banks will deteriorate, causing a slower recovery for the net worth of these intermediaries and their ability to invest. In addition, a lower aggregate quality will also imply a lower level of productive capital and output, making recessions more persistent.

In particular, given the cost function $c(\pi_t) = \frac{\tau}{2}(\pi_t^2 + \iota\pi)$, I show in the appendix that we obtain

$$\pi_t^{sb} = 2\frac{E_t\Lambda_{t,t+1}\left[R_{t+1} - \theta^B R_{t+1}^k\right]}{\left[E\Lambda_{t,t+1}\bar{\Delta}R_{t+1}^k - \frac{\tau}{2}\iota\right]} \tag{28}$$

As a result, also in this case it can be shown that both π_t^{sb} and ϕ_t^{sb} only depend on aggregate quantities, facilitating aggregation in the shadow banking sector.

At this point we can summarize the key differences between traditional banks and shadow banks in this model. First of all, shadow banks will have a higher leverage than traditional banks, achieved thanks to the possibility of pledging a larger share of the expected return on their loans. The larger amount of funds per unit of net worth that shadow banks can finance, will however be used towards lower quality projects, since $\pi_t^{sb} < \pi_t^{tb}$. Finally, the endogenous quality of loans, depending on π_t^i for $i = tb, sb$, will move countercyclically for traditional banks but procyclically for shadow banks. As we will see in the quantitative exercises, all these features point to a shadow banking system much more sensitive to aggregate negative shocks.

16

2.4 Aggregation in the Financial System

In the baseline model I assume that both types of financial intermediaries are operating, each financing a different set of projects.

As explained in detail in the next section, I follow Gertler and Karadi (2011) in assuming that each banker belongs to one of a continuum of households. In the baseline model each household will have three types of members: a worker, a traditional banker and a shadow banker. At the end of every period bankers (both traditional and shadow) exit the economy with probability $(1 - \sigma)$ and are replaced by an equal mass of workers that start their banking franchise with an initial endowment ω^j for $j = tb, sb$, according to whether they become traditional bankers or shadow bankers. As is standard in models with financial frictions, the exogenous exit probability is used to prevent net worth from growing indefinitely because of the excess returns ensuing from the agency problem.

As shown in (11) and (24), we can exploit the fact that the maximum leverage constraints are independent of individual-specific factors to aggregate across the two financial sectors. In particular, if we define N_t^j for $j = tb, fb$ as aggregate net worth, then the demand for capital in the traditional banking sector and in the shadow banking sector will be determined by

$$Q_t K_t^{tb} = \phi_t^{tb} N_t^{tb}$$

$$Q_t K_t^{sb} = \phi_t^{sb} N_t^{sb}$$

Therefore, the total capital intermediated by the financial sector is given by

$$Q_t K_t = \phi_t^{tb} N_t^{tb} + \phi_t^{sb} N_t^{sb}$$

From the equation above, we notice that the overall asset demand by banks is going to be affected by variations in both N_t^{tb} and N_t^{sb}. In particular, given the higher leverage of shadow banks, aggregate capital is going to be affected more directly by fluctuations in the net worth of non-traditional intermediaries. In addition, since π_t^{sb} and π_t^{tb} also depend only on aggregate variables, we can define the aggregate effective capital availalble for each type of financial intermediary as

$$\hat{K}_t^j = \Theta_t(\pi_{t-1}^j) K_{t-1}^j \text{ for } j = tb, sb$$

If we aggregate across surviving and entering bankers we can obtain the following evolution of the aggregate net worth for the traditional banking sector and the shadow banking sector, which comprises the retained earnings of surviving bankers, N_{st}^j, and the initial net worth of new entrants N_e^j, that is

$$N_t^j = N_{st}^j + N_e^j \text{ for } j = tb, sb$$

In particular, for each specific sector, surviving bankers' net worth will be given by the difference between the earnings on the assets held and the cost of the liabilities issued in the previous period, multiplied by the share of surviving bankers σ

$$N_{st}^j = \sigma\{Q_{t-1}\hat{K}_t^j R_t^k - R_t^j S_{t-1}^j\} \text{ for } j = tb, sb \tag{29}$$

Here we see how net worth depends on the average quality of the loans that are originated in a specific financial sector: $\Theta_t(\pi_{t-1}^j) = \pi_{t-1}^j \bar{\theta}^G + (1 - \pi_{t-1}^j)\bar{\theta}_t^B$ for $j = tb, sb$. First of all, the lower π_{t-1}^j is the more exposed to "subprime shocks" to $\bar{\theta}_t^B$ the net worth will be. In addition, a drop in the screening level at time t, will negatively affect the earnings in the next period. Furthermore, because of the higher leverage and the risk-free return on liabilities, N_t^{sb} will drop much more in response to negative shocks, as we will see in the next section.

On the other hand, the aggregate net-worth of new bankers will be simply given by their initial endowment

$$N_e^j = (1 - \sigma)\omega^j \text{ for } j = tb, sb$$

In particular, the ratio between ω^{tb} and ω^{sb}, together with leverage ratios and spreads, will be useful to determine the relative size of each financial sector in the steady state of the economy. From this perspective, this model will be agnostic about what forces determined the growth of the shadow banking system, and it will simply use a calibration where the relative size of this parallel financial system is comparable to that of the traditional banking sector. [23]

As suggested by Christiano and Ikeda (2014), this framework with endogenous probability of bank default has also implications for the cross-sectional standard deviation of banks' equity returns. Given the binomial structure of bank payoffs, the standard deviation for banks' return per unit of net worth at time t is

$$\tilde{\sigma}_{t+1}^j = \left[\pi_t^j \left(1 - \pi_t^j\right)\right]^{.5} * \phi_t^j \left[\left(\bar{\theta}^G R_{t+1}^k - b_{t+1}^{j,G}\right) - \left(\bar{\theta}^B R_{t+1}^k - b_{t+1}^{j,B}\right)\right] \text{ for } j = tb, sb$$

For traditional banks this quantity is simply

$$\tilde{\sigma}_{t+1}^{tb} = \left[\pi_t^{tb}(1 - \pi_t^{tb})\right]^{.5} \phi_t^{tb} \bar{\Delta}_{t+1} R_{t+1}^k \tag{30}$$

where the first term is decreasing in π_t^{tb} as long as $\pi_t^{tb} > .5$, which will always be the case in the calibration of the model.

On the other hand, for shadow banks, the fact that $\bar{\theta}^B R_{t+1}^k - b_{t+1}^B = 0$ implies

$$\tilde{\sigma}_{t+1}^{sb} = \left[\pi_t^{sb}(1 - \pi_t^{sb})\right]^{.5} * \phi_t^{sb} \left(\bar{\theta}^G R_{t+1}^k - b_{t+1}^{G,sb}\right)$$

and by using (23) we can write

$$\tilde{\sigma}_{t+1}^{sb} = \left[\frac{(1 - \pi_t(e_t))}{\pi_t(e_t)}\right]^{.5} \left[\phi_t^{sb} \left(\Theta\left(\pi_t^{sb}\right) R_{t+1}^k - R_{t+1}\right) + R_{t+1}\right] \tag{31}$$

where the first term is decreasing in π_t^{sb}, while the second term is increasing in the spread between shadow banks expected return on capital and the risk-free rate. Importantly, during a crisis both terms will increase. In fact, as explained above, π_t^{sb} decreases when bank net worth deteriorates and spreads rise. As a result, the agency problem of shadow banks will become more stringent, increasing the external finance premium. As can be seen from (31) these movements contribute to increase σ_{t+1}^{sb}.

Finally, the cross sectional standard deviation on the return on equity for the whole financial sector will

---

[23] One possible way to endogenize this quantity might be to assume the presence of different costs to access the shadow banking technology or the traditional banking one, in order to obtain endogenous initial inflows from households in each financial sector. Such approach is beyond the scope of this paper, but could be used as a rationale to explain the growth of shadow banking as resulting from a decrease in the cost to access alternative financial products in the years leading to the financial crisis.

be given by

$$\tilde{\sigma}_{t+1}^{fin} = \left[\left(\frac{N_t^{TB}}{\bar{N}_t} \right)^2 \left(\sigma_{t+1}^{TB} \right)^2 + \left(\frac{N_t^{SB}}{\bar{N}_t} \right)^2 \left(\sigma_{t+1}^{SB} \right)^2 \right]^{1/2} \tag{32}$$

where $\bar{N}_t = N_t^{TB} + N_t^{SB}$.

3 The Baseline Model

To capture the macroeconomic effects of shadow banking, I introduce the two types of financial intermediaries described above in a medium-scale real DSGE model. In the model there are five types of agents: households (HH), non-financial goods producers, capital producers and two types of bankers: traditional bankers (TB) and shadow bankers (SB).

Only the financial intermediaries are able to invest in productive capital by financing risky projects and they also own a unique technology allowing them to screen the quality of these assets.[24] Households can only invest by lending funds to banks. We can think of the assumption of limited market participation for households as a result of bankers technological advantage in evaluating loans.

Traditional banks and shadow banks have the same screening technology, but they differ in their "diversification technology". In fact, as described in the previous section, I assume that intermediaries operating via shadow banking are able to (partially) diversify across a pool of projects, making the ex-post realization of their portfolio more easily observable and increasing the marketability of their assets.

3.1 Households

As in Gertler and Karadi (2011), I assume that there is a representative household with a continuum of members of measure unity. Within each household there is a fraction f^w of workers, a fraction f^{tb} of "traditional bankers" and a fraction f^{sb} of "shadow bankers", where $f^w + f^{tb} + f^{sb} = 1$. In addition, I assume that the fractions of the two types of bankers are equal, so that $f^{tb} = f^{sb} = f^b$.

Workers provide labor and return wages to the household. Each type of banker manages a financial intermediary, performing the screening decision, and transfers positive dividends back to the household. There is perfect consumption insurance across household members.

Households cannot directly invest in capital, and the only way in which they can save is by lending funds to the two types of financial intermediaries. In particular, the relevant utility function for the worker is

$$\log C_t - \chi \frac{L_{t+i}^{1+\eta}}{1+\eta}$$

where C_t represents consumption and L_t labor. On the other hand, bankers utility is given by

$$\log C_t - c \left(\pi_t^j \right) Q_t k_t^j \text{ for } j = tb, sb$$

As a result, if we define $\bar{\chi} = f^w \chi$, we can write the utility of the representative household as

$$E_t \sum_{t=0}^{\infty} \beta^t \left[\log C_t - \bar{\chi} \frac{L_t^{1+\eta}}{1+\eta} - c \left(\pi_t^{tb} \right) Q_t K_t^{tb} - c \left(\pi_t^{sb} \right) Q_t K_t^{sb} \right]$$

---

[24]From now on I will use the words "projects", "capital" and "loans" interchangeably

As described in the previous section, the financial system offers two types of securities to outside investors. Shadow banks offer securities , S_t^{sb}, that pay a risk-free return, $R_{t+1}^{sb} = R_{t+1}$ in case a run on the SB-system does not occur. Since I am modeling the variety of institutions that composed the SB-system as a single entity, we can think of S_t^{sb} as representing the set of instruments that allowed investors to channel funds into this parallel banking sector. For example we can refer to asset backed commercial paper (ABCP) or shares of money market mutual funds (MMMFS), that in normal times were perceived as basically risk-free assets. What is important is that lenders are paid according to a "sequential service constraint", so that if shadow banks do not have sufficient resources to repay all creditors, the latter have an incentive to withdraw their funds as soon as possible. In the model, I assume that a run on the SB-system is a completely unanticipated event, so that I can characterize the household problem and the subsequent optimal contracts with the financial intermediaries as if households do not expect a run event to occur next period.

Traditional banks issue liabilities S_t^{tb}, that pay a return R_{t+1}^{tb} that is exposed to aggregate fluctuations. Because of the structure of this security, traditional banks will always be able to repay the promised return on S_t^{tb}. Even if I am not directly modelling a government-backed deposit insurance, the microfoundation for the funding problem of traditional banks will endogenously imply that they are not exposed to a bank run.

The budget constraint for households is given by

$$C_t^h + S_t^{tb} + S_t^{sb} = R_t^{tb} S_{t-1}^{tb} + R_t^{sb} S_{t-1}^{sb} + \Pi_t + W_t L_t \tag{33}$$

where W_t represents real wage and Π_t are profits derived from the ownership of capital-producing firms.

The first order conditions for the choice of assets and and labor are given by

$$E_t \Lambda_{t,t+1} R_{t+1}^j = 1 \text{ for } j = tb, sb \tag{34}$$

$$C_t^{-1} W_t = \bar{\chi} L_t^\eta \tag{35}$$

where $\Lambda_{t,t+1} = \beta \frac{C_t}{C_{t+1}}$.

3.2   Physical Setup

As was shown above, all the traditional banks will choose the same π_t^{tb} and all the shadow banks will choose the same π_t^{sb} so that if we define the aggregate capital financed by one financial sector at time t as K_t^j for $j = tb, sb$, then the effective capital available for production in each financial system will be

$$\hat{K}_t^j = \Theta_t(\pi_{t-1}^j) K_{t-1}^j \text{ for } j = tb, sb \tag{36}$$

and consequently, aggregate effective capital will be

$$\hat{K}_t = \hat{K}_t^{tb} + \hat{K}_t^{sb}$$

After the idiosyncratic default realization, projects become homogeneous raw capital again. Therefore, if we denote by I_t aggregate investment and by δ the rate of exogenous physical depreciation, then the evolution of aggregate capital $K_t = K_t^{tb} + K_t^{sb}$, will be given by

$$K_t = (1 - \delta)\hat{K}_t + I_t \tag{37}$$

In addition, it will also be useful to define the following measure for aggregate screening $\hat{\pi}_t$, which weights the monitoring level of each type of bank by the share of capital intermediated

$$\hat{\pi}_t = \pi_t^{tb} \frac{K_t^{tb}}{K_t} + \pi_t^{sb} \frac{K_t^{sb}}{K_t}$$

Therefore, we can define "aggregate quality" as

$$\hat{\Theta}_t \left(\hat{\pi}_{t-1} \right) = \frac{\hat{K}_t}{K_{t-1}}$$

At this point, comparing this setup with that of Gertler and Karadi (2011), we can think of $\hat{\Theta}_t(\hat{\pi}_{t-1})$ as a way to endogenize the "capital quality shock" used in their paper, which affects the amount of capital available for production in every period.

3.3   Non-Financial Firms

In the model there are two types of non-financial firms: goods producers and capital producers.

3.3.1   Goods Producers

Goods producers operate a Cobb-Douglas production function with effective capital and labor, under perfect competition. Since labor is perfectly mobile across islands we can write aggregate output Y_t as a function of aggregate productive capital, $\hat{K}_t$, and aggregate labor L_t

$$Y_t = A_t \hat{K}_t^\alpha L_t^{1-\alpha} \tag{38}$$

where $\alpha \in (0,1)$ and A_t is aggregate productivity.

Given the effective capital available for production, firms choose labor in order to satisfy

$$W_t = (1 - \alpha) \frac{Y_t}{L_t} \tag{39}$$

so that we can define gross profits per unit of effective capital as

$$Z_t = \frac{Y_t - W_t L_t}{\hat{K}_t} = \alpha \frac{Y_t}{\hat{K}_t} \tag{40}$$

Firms finance the purchase of capital/projects every period by obtaining funds from financial intermediaries. As in Gertler and Karadi (2011), I assume that there are no frictions in the relationship between banks and goods producers. Banks can perfectly observe the realization (θ_L, θ_H) of projects purchased by a firm in a given island and can efficiently enforce contractual obligations with these borrowers. As a result, goods producers can issue state contingent claims that are a claim to future returns from one unit of investments. Because of perfect competition, the price of these securities will be the same price of investment goods Q_t.

It is important to notice that, because of perfect labor mobility and constant returns to scale, we do not need to keep track of the distribution of default shocks, and consequently of effective capital, across islands. This allows us to consider a return per loan for an individual bank that is linear in expected quality, that is

$E_t \Theta_{t+1} \left(\pi_t^i \right) R_{t+1}^k$ for $i = tb, sb$, where

$$R_{t+1}^k = \frac{Z_{t+1} + (1 - \delta) Q_{t+1}}{Q_t}$$

3.3.2 Capital Producers

Capital producers create new capital by using the final good as input and face convex adjustment costs in the gross rate of change in investment, $f \left(\frac{I_t}{I_{t-1}} \right) I_t$, where $f(1) = f'(1) = 0$ and $f''() > 0$. They sell new "raw" capital to firms in the different islands at the price Q_t.

Given that households own capital producers, they choose I_t to maximize the following

$$\max_{I_\tau} \sum_{\tau=t}^{\infty} \beta^{\tau-t} \Lambda_{t,\tau+1} \left\{ Q_t I_\tau - I_\tau - f(\frac{I_\tau}{I_{\tau-1}}) I_\tau \right\}$$

so that the price of capital will be determined by

$$Q_t = 1 + f \left(\frac{I_t}{I_{t-1}} \right) + \frac{I_t}{I_{t-1}} f' \left(\frac{I_t}{I_{t-1}} \right) - E_t \beta \Lambda_{t,t+1} \left(\frac{I_{t+1}}{I_t} \right)^2 f' \left(\frac{I_{t+1}}{I_t} \right)$$

Profits, arising out of the steady state, are redistributed lump sum to households.

3.4 Equilibrium in the Baseline Model without Runs

To close the baseline model (in which we abstract from government intervention and runs on the SB-system) we need to specify the equilibrium in the labor market and the aggregate resource constraint. In particular, labor demand and labor supply will be equalized if the following holds

$$C_t^{-1}(1 - \alpha) \frac{Y_t}{L_t} = \chi L_t^{\eta}$$

Aggregate output is divided between household consumption C_t, and investment expenditures I_t

$$Y_t = C_t + \left[1 + f \left(\frac{I_t}{I_{t-1}} \right) \right] I_t \tag{41}$$

The exogenous processes for productivity A_t, and monitoring cost τ_t, each follow an AR(1) process

$$A_t = (1 - \rho_A) A^{SS} + \rho_A A_{t-1} + \varepsilon_t^A$$

$$\tau_t = (1 - \rho_\tau) \tau^{SS} + \rho_\tau A_{t-1} + \varepsilon_t^\tau$$

whereas I assume that the default rate of bad loans p_t^B follows an i.i.d. process and is not correlated with $\varepsilon_t^A, \varepsilon_t^\tau$.

4   A Run on the Shadow Banking System

In this framework, the possibility of having two types of financial intermediaries financing investment expenditures can cause the occurrence of an alternative equilibrium characterized by a run on the shadow banking system. In particular, in a run scenario, households stop rolling over their debt with existing shadow banks. As a result, in order to repay their creditors, existing shadow banks have to sell their assets to traditional banks and entering shadow banks. In particular, the latter start operating with their small endowment ω^{sb} and no pre-existing debt, and hence are not exposed to runs in the period. If the fire-sale value of these assets, arising from the re-intermediation towards banks with low leverage capacity (TB) or very low net worth (entering SB), is low enough, a run equilibrium that wipes out existing shadow banks will be possible. After the run occurs, new shadow banks will accumulate net worth until the economy slowly transitions back to the steady state.

As in Gertler and Kiyotaki (2013), I assume that at time $t-1$ the run is a zero probability event for the agents in the economy. At time t households will decide whether to continue to provide funds to the existing shadow bankers or not. Therefore, the run equilibrium will exist together with the "normal" equilibrium in which agents keep lending to shadow banks. For this reason the possibility of a run is not taken into account when deriving the optimal contracts in section 2.

A run equilibrium will be possible if investors believe that, if all households stop providing funds to shadow banks, then the SB-system might not be able to satisfy all its creditors. Therefore, if we assume some type of sequential service on the repayments from shadow banks liabilities, then all households have the incentive to withdraw their funds in order to avoid being left with nothing.

As noted earlier, given the contract structure for traditional banks, a run on the TB-system will never be possible in this framework. By introducing some changes to the contractual framework we could also allow for this event, however the focus of this paper is on studying a run phenomenon similar to the one that occurred during the great recession, and that mainly affected the shadow banking sector.[25]

4.1 Conditions for a Run

As a first step to characterize the run equilibrium, we can determine a threshold value for the price of capital $\bar{Q}_t$, below which a run on shadow banks is feasible. In particular, the events of a run happen as follows. At the beginning of time t, households decide whether to roll over their ABCP or not. If they choose to run, the assets of all existing shadow banks are sold to the TB sector and to entering SBs, and the amount obtained is transferred to households. Define Q_t^* as the liquidation price realized in this case. Then, a run will be possible if the liquidation value of the assets of the SB system is smaller than the claim of creditors, that is

$$(Z_t + (1-\delta)Q_t^*)\Theta_t(\pi_{t-1}^{sb})K_{t-1}^{sb} < S_{t-1}^{sb}R_t \qquad (42)$$

At the individual bank level, given the contract between shadow banks and households, condition (42) is equivalent to having a return on capital in case of a run, R_t^{k*}, so low that the payment to households, b_t^G, implied by the participation constraint (20) would have to be higher than $\bar{\theta}^G R_t^{k*}$, violating limited liability. That is, a run is possible if the price of assets is so low that even the shadow banks with a good realization for their pool of loans would not be able to repay creditors.

When the condition above is satisfied, all investors have the incentive to run in order to avoid being left with zero after the run occurs. Notice that equation (42) can be equivalently stated as the condition such

---

[25] For example we could assume that payments promised by the commercial banks depend on the price of the economy without a run Q_t, so that there could be the possibility for the net worth of commercial banks to turn negative as well.

However, given the lower leverage of TBs and the high leverage capacity of SBs a TB-run scenario in which SBs continue operating seems quantitatively unfeasible, unless we also introduce some type of costly technology that allows households to directly invest in capital as in Gertler and Kiyotaki (2013).

that the aggregate net worth of the shadow banking system, not considering new entrants, becomes negative, that is

$$(Z_t + (1 - \delta)Q_t^*)\Theta_t(\pi_{t-1}^{sb})K_{t-1}^{sb} - Q_{t-1}K_{t-1}^{sb}R_t < N_t^{sb}R_t$$

By using the balance sheet and the leverage equation for shadow banks, we can rewrite this condition as

$$Q_t^* < \bar{Q}_t$$

$$\text{where } \bar{Q}_t = \frac{1}{1 - \delta}\left[\frac{R_t}{\Theta_t(\pi_{t-1}^{sb})}\left(1 - \frac{1}{\phi_{t-1}^{sb}}\right)Q_{t-1} - Z_t\right] \tag{43}$$

From this relationship, we can analyze how the possibility of a run depends on different endogenous economic variables. In particular, all the variables contributing to an increase in $\bar{Q}_t$ will increase the measure of states in which a run is possible. Similarly to Gertler and Kiyotaki (2013), $\bar{Q}_t$ will be higher when the leverage of shadow banks, ϕ_{t-1}^{sb}, is higher. In addition, a feature unique to this setup is that $\bar{Q}_t$ will also be decreasing in $\Theta_t(\pi_{t-1}^{sb})$, the average quality of loans intermediated by the SB-system. This means that if the quality of the assets intermediated by shadow banks starts deteriorating then the possibility of a run will become greater. Such mechanism might have played an important role in igniting the run on several components of the shadow banking system as the foreclosure rate on subprime securities began to surge.

Alternatively, given $\bar{Q}_t$ and Q_t^*, we can characterize the possibility of a run by computing the recovery rate on SB assets, that is

$$\bar{\gamma}_t = \frac{\Theta_t(\pi_{t-1}^{sb})(Z_t + (1 - \delta)Q_t^*)K_{t-1}^{sb}}{S_{t-1}^{sb}R_t}$$

Consequently, if $\bar{\gamma}_t > 1$ an ex-post run will not be possible. This quantity can also be interpreted as the fraction of "alert" withdrawing depositors needed for a run to be possible.

We can now turn to the determination of the liquidation price, Q_t^*. As mentioned above, I assume that at the time of a successful run, once the existing shadow banks are liquidated, only traditional banks and entering shadow banks will be able to intermediate capital. It is important to note that, unlike Gertler and Kiyotaki (2014), a run event does not entail any additional output cost, but will have real consequences because of the drop in investments caused by the collapse of the shadow banking system. Given the features of the run equilibrium, it is easy to characterize the economy when a run occurs. In fact, the only modification needed is to set the net worth of surviving shadow bankers to zero, so that

$$N_t^{sb*} = N_e^{sb} = (1 - \sigma)\omega^{sb}$$

As a result, at the time of the run, the shadow banking sector's ability to intermediate funds will be dramatically affected, since its net worth will fall almost to zero. Consequently, if the run occurs during a crisis, the traditional banking sector will have to absorb a substantially larger amount of capital compared to an equilibrium in which a run does not materialize. This will be crucial for the drop in Q_t that will make a run possible. Moreover, a drop in the price of capital will also affect the net worth of traditional banks, making the liquidation price even lower and a run more likely.

5 Numerical Exercises

The quantitative exercises in this section are meant to illustrate how the introduction of the shadow banking system makes the economy more fragile, compared to a framework where only TB operate, the Traditional Banking Economy (TBE), or one where there are no informational asymmetries, the Frictionless Economy (FE). The impulse responses provided are the non-linear perfect foresight paths of the economy, in order to capture the non-linearities arising especially when the endogenous state variables move far from the steady state levels, as it occurs when a run takes place.

5.1 Calibration

Table 1 reports the parameters used for the baseline model. Out of the fifteen parameters of the model, the seven parameters pertaining to preferences and technology are fairly standard. I use a discount factor $\beta = .99$, a utility weight on labor $\bar{\chi} = 2$ and a Frisch elasticity of 1. The capital share α is set at 0.36, the exogenous depreciation rate is 2.5% and the elasticity of the price of capital to investments, given by f'', is set at 2.3.

The remaining parameters are specific to my model. I assume $\sigma = 0.9$, which implies that the average life of bankers is 10 quarters. In addition, I normalize $p^H = 1$, and I calibrate the other seven parameters specific to the banking sector, $\theta_L, \theta_H, p^b, \tau, \iota, \omega^{tb}, \omega^{sb}$ to hit the following targets: a shadow bank leverage of 12 compared to a leverage for traditional banks of 4; a level of π^{sb} equal to 0.95 and π^{tb} equal to 0.975; a steady-state quarterly spread of the return of capital over the risk free rate of 40 basis points, an aggregate quality $\Theta(\hat{\pi})$ equal to 1 (a normalization), and a share of aggregate capital intermediated by shadow banks equal to .5 .

The values for ϕ^{tb} and ϕ^{sb} are meant to capture the difference in leverage between traditional banks (leverage around 10) and broker dealers (leverage above 30) in the period preceding the financial crisis. The aggregate levels of leverage are below the actual ones for financial intermediaries because in this model banks are directly investing in the equity of the goods producers, and non-financial firms typically have a much lower leverage.

The values for the screening levels are meant to capture a delinquency rate for the loans of traditional banks, $1 - \pi^{tb} = 2.5\%$, similar to the delinquency rate of prime mortgages. On the other hand the implied delinquency rate for loans originated by shadow banks is twice as large at 5%, and is a conservative estimate of the delinquency rate of subprimes.[26]

Finally, the spread on the return on capital is supposed to be a combination of the average spread on mortgage backed securities, around 100bp annually, and the Baa-treasury spread on corporate bonds, which was larger than 2% annually.

Given these parameters, in table 2 I also report the implied steady state values for the "Frictionless Economy" (FE), where financial frictions are absent, and the "Traditional Banking Economy" (TBE) where the only type of financial intermediaries present are traditional banks.[27] From table 2, we see how the introduction of shadow banks increases capital (by 20%), output (by 8%) and consumption (by 3%) with respect to the TBE, even if loan quality is lower. On the other hand the baseline economy implies lower values for these variables, when compared to the frictionless one.

---

[26] Delinquency rates on adjustable rate mortgages (ARM) were above 10% in 2005.

[27] In particular, in this case I assume that the transfer to traditional banks is equal to the total transfer to the financial sector in the baseline economy, that is $\omega^{tbe} = \omega^{tb} + \omega^{sb}$.

In addition, if we measure these differences in terms of the change in consumption that would equalize the steady state utilities across the different economies, we have that the introduction of shadow banks provides a consumption equivalent gain of 3.6% but it falls short of the frictionless economy by about .02%.[28]

5.2 Crisis experiments

In this set of examples I compare the response of the baseline economy (solid line), in the no-run equilibrium, with the response of the traditional banking economy (red dashed line) and of the frictionless economy (green dotted line) to the same shock.

As a first experiment, I consider a 1% drop in productivity with a persistence of 0.95. Figure (3) reports the results for the different economies. In the baseline model, the drop in A_t negatively affects the net worth of both banks. As a result, because of the tightening in their balance sheet, banks will have to sell their assets, depressing asset prices and further affecting the net worth of financial intermediaries. This sequence of events is in line with the financial accelerator mechanism described in Gertler and Karadi (2011) and other macroeconomic papers with financial frictions. However, there are several aspects of a crisis that are unique to this setup.

First, we notice that during the downturn, traditional banks' asset holdings increase by about 8%, whereas projects funded by shadow banks decrease by about 12%. This is similar to the reintermediation of credit that I have described in the introduction. In fact, because of their higher initial leverage, the decline in net worth will make the financial constraint of shadow banks more binding, so that they will have to offload assets to the other financial sector. However, because of their lower leverage capacity, for traditional banks to be able to absorb the capital held by shadow banks, prices need to adjust downward. This amplifies the financial accelerator channel, resulting in an initial drop in N_t^{sb} of about 25%, and a prolonged reintermediation as we can see from the evolution of K_t^{tb} and K_t^{sb} in the graph. Consequently, aggregate investments and prices decrease, causing a slower recovery of the capital stock in the economy.

An additional variable that is going to determine the recovery of the economy is the endogenous quality of loans. As we can see in the bottom-right part of figure (3), π_t^{sb} decreases by more than 7% on impact, whereas π_t^{tb} increases by about 0.5%. As explained in section 2, these opposite movements are a consequence of the different contract structures. Given the drop in prices and the higher expected return on capital, traditional banks find it optimal to increase their screening effort. On the other hand, the considerable deterioration in shadow banks net worth decreases the "skin in the game" that they can credibly promise to investors, implying a lower level of screening.

The lower quality of loans intermediated by shadow banks during a recession makes the crisis more persistent for two reasons. First, it causes a slower recovery for N_t^{sb}, because of the implied lower average return in the shadow banking sector. In addition, since the drop in π_t^{sb} is larger than the increase in π_t^{tb}, the "aggregate quality" of capital, $\hat{\Theta}$, deteriorates by about .3%. As a result, effective capital falls, contributing to a slower recovery of output.

Importantly, this effect is basically absent when we consider the other two types of economy. If we compare the path of the baseline economy with the TB economy and the Frictionless economy, we see that the productivity shock has larger consequences when shadow banks are present. One reason for this is the lower aggregate leverage in the economy with only traditional banks. This implies a weaker financial

---

[28]It has to be noted that a proper welfare evaluation would require to solve the model globally accounting also for the frequency of crises arising from the binding incentive constraints. However this is beyond the scope of this paper and is left for further research.

accelerator, as evidenced by the fact that the drop in prices is about 80% smaller than in the baseline economy. In addition, in the traditional banking economy there is no deterioration in asset quality during a recession. As a consequence, the net worth of traditional banks suffers a moderate drop and recovers relatively quickly, and the decrease in aggregate capital and labor (not reported) is about one fourth of that experienced in the baseline economy. The TB-economy behaves similarly to the frictionless economy because of the low leverage and the absence of interaction between loan quality and funding capacity. However it has to be remembered that, as shown in Table 2, the steady state values of consumption and output are substantially lower in the traditional banking economy.

Next, I consider a "subprime shock" that affects only the average quality of bad loans, $\bar{\theta}_t^B$. In particular I consider an increase in the default rate in the bad region (a decrease in p_t^B), with no persistence, that causes a 10% drop in $\bar{\theta}_t^B$. We can think of this experiment as the initial rise in subprime defaults that ignited the financial crisis.

The results of this experiment are reported in figure (4). Given that bad loans represent only a small portion of total projects, the drop in the aggregate quality of effective capital at time t, $\hat{\Theta}_t$ is only .3%, so that this can be considered as a relatively small "capital quality shock" as the one used by Gertler and Karadi (2011) or Gertler and Kiyotaki (2010). In this case, the initial shock hits the net worth of shadow banks more directly because of the higher exposure to bad projects. Once the financing conditions of banks become tighter, we will have all the same mechanisms described in the previous experiment: the financial accelerator, the reintermediation, and the deterioration of the quality of projects financed by the SB-system. As a consequence, aggregate capital declines up to 1% so that output and consumption experience a prolonged decline, despite the absence of persistence in the shock.

If we consider the responses in the traditional banking economy and the frictionless economy, we see that the difference from the baseline economy is even larger than in the previous experiment. First of all, the initial impact on existing effective capital is about 50% larger in the shadow banking economy, as can be seen from the different drops in $\hat{\Theta}_t$, because of the larger proportion of bad loans financed.

In addition, since the shock is i.i.d, this experiment captures in a stark way the slower recovery caused by shadow intermediaries. In fact, in the economy with only traditional banks, the financial sector is more stable both because of the lower leverage and because bank liabilities are contingent on the aggregate state. Consequently, after the initial shock to N_t^{tb}, the economy is able to quickly restore capital by increasing investments, so that prices are almost unchanged. As a result, at the trough, the drop in output and consumption is less than one-tenth of the one occurring in the baseline economy.

Finally, figure (5) presents the evolution of the cross sectional volatily of equity returns in the financial sector, for each shock. The first thing to notice is the spike in $\tilde{\sigma}_{t+1}^{sb}$, which increases by 65% with the tfp shock and 40% with the subprime shock. Looking at equation (31), we can see that this is due to three effects, all resulting from a deterioration in N_t^{sb}: the drop in π_t^{sb}, the increase in leverage, ϕ_t^{sb}, and the higher expected return from capital (due to the tightening of the incentive constraint).

On the other hand, $\tilde{\sigma}_{t+1}^{tb}$ is characterized by a much smaller movement in the opposite direction, due to the opposing movements in π_t^{sb}, ϕ_t^{tb} and $E_t\Lambda_{t,t+1}R_{t+1}^k$, as can be seen from equation (30). As a result, the standard deviation in the whole financial sector increases in both experiments, as it occurred at the peak of the financial crisis.

5.3   An Increase in the Screening Cost

After analyzing how the different banking systems react to real disturbances, we can now focus on shocks that directly interact with the nature of the financial frictions. Figure (6) shows the effect of an unanticipated 5% increase in the variable τ_t, which implies a higher marginal cost of screening projects for both banks, with a persistence of .5.

As can be seen from (13) and (28), the immediate effect of such a shock is a drop in both π_t^{tb} and π_t^{sb}, due to the fact that monitoring is now more costly for banks. In the TB-system this is the only effect that takes place.

However, in the shadow banking system, the higher cost of monitoring will also make the UE-friction more severe, because now the cost to provide incentives to bankers will be higher. This will imply a negative pressure on the maximum leverage constraint for shadow banks, as described in (24), so that shadow banks will have to start selling their assets. As a result, spreads will increase and current prices will drop generating all the amplification effects described in the previous experiments. The interaction of τ_t with shadow banks leverage implies that π_t^{sb} drops about 1% more than π_t^{tb}. In addition, the recovery in aggregate quality is slower in the baseline model, because it is also driven by a slower recovery of prices.

Interestingly, even if this shock does not have any real consequences on impact, it causes output and consumption to drop up to 0.3% and consumption up to .4% . In the traditional banking economy, the only effect comes from the initial drop in π, which however quickly returns to the steady state level, since prices and investments stay almost unchanged. As a result, output experiences a contraction 50% smaller than in the baseline model.

5.4   A Wealth Transfer Within the Financial System

In order to illustrate the relevance of the different leverage capacities of the two financial sectors and the consequences of reintermediation, I consider a simple experiment in the baseline model that consists in a transfer from the net worth of shadow banks to the one of traditional banks. In particular, figure (7) shows the effects of a transfer T equal to 1% of the steady state level of N_t^{sb}.

Given the lower leverage of traditional banks, the amount of funds that can be intermediated with T units of internal funds is lower in the traditional banking sector than in the shadow banking one. As a result, aggregate investments decline igniting a drop in prices and the consequent amplification mechanisms present in the baseline model, implying fire sales and a decline in aggregate loan quality. Given the drop in Q_t, the actual initial drop in N_t^{sb} is actually larger than 1%.

The real effects of reintermediation will play an important role in the run experiment that I consider in the next subsection.

5.5   A Run Experiment

During the financial crisis, investors stopped considering some of the securities issued by the shadow banking system as substitutes for risk-free assets. This caused a run first on the ABCP market and then on the MMMFs. To model the consequences of these events, I now allow for the possibility of a run on the shadow banking system.

Given the liquidation price, Q_t^*, and the threshold, $\bar{Q}_t$, determined in (43), a run will be possible in the baseline model at time t if and only if

$$Run_t = \bar{Q}_t - Q_t^* > 0$$

The model calibration implies that a run equilibrium is not possible in steady state. However, during a recession $\bar{Q}_t$ will increase and Q_t^* will decrease, so that the quantity Run_t will indicate whether a run is feasible after a shock hits the economy.

First, I consider a run occurring after a tfp shock. In addition, in line with the narrative of the recent financial crisis, I also consider the eventuality of a run happening after an increase in the default rate of riskier loans. In particular, I consider the same shock magnitudes as in figures (3) and (4).

Figure (10) shows how, after the initial shock is realized, a run becomes possible for four periods in both cases. In figure (8) and (9), I compare the path of the economy when the run happens in the third period (the dashed red line) to the same response of the baseline economy (solid blue line) when a run does not occur. Both lines are deviations from the steady state of the baseline economy.

When the run occurs, traditional banks absorb most of the capital of defaulting shadow banks. As a result, the capital holding of traditional banks increases much more dramatically in this case. Due to the low leverage capacity of traditional banks, in order for them to be able to intermediate such a higher amount of capital, prices need to drop by almost 10%, instead of the much smaller drop that would have occurred without a run. It is this drop in Q_t that makes the run possible. At the time of the run, the net worth of shadow banks drops by more than 95%, causing a much slower recovery for this financial sector. The considerably larger decrease in asset prices and N_t^{sb} implies a noticeable amplification of all the feedback mechanisms that I have described in the previous set of experiments. In fact, in both figure 7 and figure 8, after a run occurs investment drops by more than 10% and asset quality by more than 1.5%, implying a decrease of output and consumption at the trough of more than 2%. In addition, the decrease in prices negatively affects the net worth of the surviving traditional banks, impairing their ability to invest and further reducing prices. Interestingly, as figure 9 shows, the possibility of a bank run can create a deep and prolonged recession even after a relatively small shock like the subprime one.

In both cases, the initial increase in consumption occurring at the time of the run is due to the fact that households are not able to invest in the TB-system all the funds that they have withdrawn from the SB-system. This path for consumption is consistent with that observed during the financial crisis.

6 Government Intervention

In this section, I consider the possibility that the government is willing to facilitate lending by directly purchasing securities in the asset market, similarly to some of the unconventional policies that the Fed put in place during the financial crisis. Define the total amount of assets that are privately intermediated by the financial sector as $K_t^p = K_t^{tb} + K_t^{sb}$. Therefore, if the government funds an amount K_t^g, the total value of assets will be

$$Q_t K_t = Q_t K_t^p + Q_t K_t^g$$

The government can fund itself frictionlessly by issuing risk-free bonds, D_t^g, but it does not have the monitoring technology owned by the banking sector. In particular, I assume that the government's projects will have a fixed quality $\bar{\pi}$. It is also important to assume that the goverment will be able to diversify also across regions. On the other hand, as in Gertler and Karadi (2011), I assume that government intermediation causes efficiency costs proportional to the amount funded, $\xi Q_t K_t^g$.

If we define T_t as government transfers, the government's budget constraint will be

$$\xi Q_t K_t^g + Q_t K_t^g + R_t D_{t-1}^g = D_t^g + \Theta_t(\bar{\pi}) R_t^k Q_{t-1} K_{t-1}^g + T_t$$

and if we assume that at every period the government is going to fund its asset purchases through risk-free bonds then $D_t^g = Q_t K_t^g$, so that we can rewrite the budget constraint as

$$\xi Q_t K_t^g = T_t + \left[\Theta_t(\bar{\pi}) R_t^k - R_t\right] Q_{t-1} K_{t-1}^g$$

To characterize government policy, I assume that the central bank intermediates a fraction ψ_t of total assets,

$$K_t^g = \psi_t K_t$$

To model ψ_t, I assume that the government intervenes when spreads $\left(E_t R_{t+1}^k - R_{t+1}\right)$ rise. In fact, this will occur during a crisis, when prices drop and financial frictions are tighter. In particular, I consider the following simple rule for government intervention

$$\psi_t = \begin{cases} \psi_1 \left\{E_t \left[\Theta_{t+1}(\bar{\pi}) R_{t+1}^k - R_{t+1}\right]\right\} & \text{if} \left\{E_t \left[\Theta_{t+1}(\bar{\pi}) R_{t+1}^k - R_{t+1}\right]\right\} > 0 \\ 0 & \text{otherwise} \end{cases} \tag{44}$$

where I parameterize $\bar{\pi}$ in such a way that $E_t \left[\Theta_{t+1}(\bar{\pi}) R_{t+1}^k - R_{t+1}\right]$ is zero in the steady state of the baseline model. This implies that $\bar{\pi} < \pi^{sb} < \pi^{tb}$. Therefore, the government will start intermediating assets only when it makes a positive excess expected returnn. The parameter ψ_1 will determine the intensity of the government reaction.

6.1 Crisis Experiment with Government Intervention

Figure 11 and 12 show the response of the baseline economy to the same shocks considered in figure (3) and (4), when the credit policy is in place. The parameter ψ_1 is set to 5 (or to 20), so that the government intermediates 2% (or 3%) of assets when the tfp shock hits and 1.5% (2%) when the subprime shock occurs; the inefficiency parameter ξ is set for now at .0025.

By intervening in the asset market, the central bank initially prevents the reintermediation from shadow banks to traditional banks. In this way, government intervention contains the drop in prices, causing a faster recovery in the net worth of shadow banks and reducing the initial deterioration in asset quality. The impact of central bank credit intermediation on the endogenous quality of assets is a novel mechanism of this paper, highlighting an additional positive effect of government intervention during a crisis. Under this policy, the drop in output and consumption is up to 50% smaller at the trough than in the baseline model.

6.2 Run Experiment with Government Intervention

In this framework, it is interesting to investigate how government intervention interacts with the possibility of a run. Even if the run is unanticipated, I can look at the fraction of "alert" investors, $\bar{\gamma}_t$, necessary for a run to be possible, as an indicator of the exposure of the economy to a run on the SB-system. In particular, I assume that the government policy described above, is in place also in the run equilibrium. The idea is that now, at the time of the run, investors know that the government will act in order to increase the leverage capacity of the financial system, whether this is composed only of traditional banks or of both types of financial intermediaries.

In figure (13) I consider the same run experiments analyzed before, for different levels of government interventions ψ_1, and plot the implied $\bar{\gamma}_t$. This exercise is performed for three different levels of efficiency costs, ξ: 0, 0.0025 and 0.005.

As ψ_1 increases, the fraction of investors needed for a run to be possible increases as well, and if $\xi = 0$, a run is not possible already with ψ_1 around 5. The intuition for this result is that if a central bank absorbs part of the assets of SBs, then the liquidation price will be higher in the event of a run. On the other hand, as ξ increases, the government is less effective in containing the drop in Q_t^*, and fewer alert agents are necessary to have a run. In particular, the parameter ξ can be thought of as either the cost that the central bank has to face to (imperfectly) replicate the unique monitoring technology that banks have, in order to achieve a $\bar{\pi} > 0$, or as the cost for diversifying across islands. The key feature of this experiment is that it captures how, the fact that the Fed tried to replace the private demand for different types of asset-backed securities probably also helped to prevent additional run episodes on "shadow intermediaries".

7 Conclusion

There is no univocal definition for the term "shadow banking", since it encompasses a variety of financial markets and institutions that are interconnected in very complex ways. In this paper, I try to capture some of the salient features of this alternative banking system that played a significant role in the recent crisis. In particular, I show how financial innovation and higher diversification, which were at the heart of the "originate-to-distribute" model, can make the real economy more fragile in different ways. First, the SB-system increases the aggregate leverage of the financial sector, amplifying exogenous shocks. In addition, it reduces banks' incentives to invest in high quality loans, increasing their exposure to "subprime shocks" and causing procyclical asset quality. Furthermore, I also perform an experiment involving a run on the shadow banking system, aimed at replicating the events that caused turmoil in the markets for ABCP and MMMF shares. As the exercise shows, if a run occurs, the shutdown of the markets for securities on which the modern financial system heavily relies can have long-lasting consequences for real investment, output, and consumption. Finally, I show that there is scope for government intervention. In fact, by directly purchasing assets that were previously intermediated by the SB-system, the central bank can intervene on the reintermediation process, from shadow banks to traditional banks, that is responsible for the drop in asset prices during a crisis. As a result, such policies can dampen the effects of a recession and even prevent a run on the SB-system.

This framework could be used to study other important policies aimed at improving financial stability. For example, a leverage restriction similar to the one considered by Christiano and Ikeda (2014) could have the twofold benefit of providing incentives for bank screening of projects and directly reducing the likelihood of a run, as suggested by Gertler and Kiyotaki (2014).

References

[1] Acharya, Viral V., Philipp Schnabl, and Gustavo Suarez (forthcoming) "Securitization without risk transfer,"Journal of Financial Economics

[2] Adrian, Tobias and Adam B. Ashcraft, "Shadow Banking: A Review of Literature",Federal Reserve Bank of New York, Staff Report No. 580.

[3] Angeloni, I., and E. Faia, 2013, Capital Regulation and Monetary Policy with Fragile Banks, Journal of Monetary Policy 60, 3111-382.

[4] Allen, F., and Gale, D., 2007. Understanding Financial Crises. Oxford University Press.

[5] Bernanke, B., and Gertler, M., 1989. Agency Costs, Net Worth and Business Fluctuations. American Economic Review 79, 14-31.

[6] Bigio, S., 2012. Financial Risk Capacity. Mimeo, Columbia Business School.

[7] Brunnermeier, M. K., and Sannikov, Y., 2011. "A Macroeconomic Model with a Financial Sector", American Economic Review, 104(2), 379-421

[8] Christiano, L. and Ikeda D., 2014, "Leverage Restrictions in a Business Cycle Model". Macroeconomic and Financial Stability: Challenges for Monetary Policy, Conference Volumn, XVI Annual Conference of the Central Bank of Chile

[9] Christiano, Motto and Rostagno , 2015, "Risk Shocks", American Economic Review

[10] Covitz, Daniel, Nellie Liang, and Gustavo A. Suarez (2013). "The Evolution of a Financial Crisis: Collapse of the Asset-Backed Commercial Paper Market," Journal of Finance, vol. 68, no. 3, pp. 815-848

[11] DeMarzo, Peter M. (2005) "The pooling and tranching of securities: A model of informed intermediation," Review of Financial Studies, Vol. 18, pp. 1–35.

[12] Diamond, D., and Dybvig, P., 1983. Bank Runs, Deposit Insurance, and Liquidity. Journal of Political Economy 91, 401-419.

[13] Diamond, D., and Rajan, R., 2000. A Theory of Bank Capital, Journal of Finance

[14] Drucker, Steven and Puri Manju, (2009), "On Loan Sales, Loan Contracting and Lending Relationships", Review of Financial Studies, 22, 2835-2872.

[15] Faia, Ester, 2010. "Credit risk transfers and the macroeconomy," Working Paper Series 1256, European Central Bank

[16] Ferreira, Thiago R. T. 2014. "Financial Volatility and Economic Activity." Unpublished, Northwestern University.

[17] Gennaioli, Nicola, Andrei Shleifer, and Robert Vishny 2013. (forthcoming) "A model of shadow banking," Journal of Finance

[18] Gertler, M., and Karadi, P., 2011. A Model of Unconventional Monetary Policy, Journal of Monetary Economics, January

[19] Gertler, M., and Kiyotaki, N., 2010. Financial Intermediation and Credit Policy in Business Cycle Analysis. In Friedman, B., and Woodford, M. (Eds.), Handbook of Monetary Economics. Elsevier, Amsterdam, Netherlands

[20] Gertler, M., and Kiyotaki, N., 2013. Banking, Liquidity and Bank Runs in an Infinite Horizon Economy, mimeo

[21] Gorton, G., 2010. Slapped by the Invisible Hand: The Panic of 2007. Oxford University Press.

[22] Gorton, Gary and Andrew Metrick (2012a) "Securitized banking and the run on repo," Journal of Financial Economics , Vol. 104, pp. 425–451

[23] He. Z. and A. Krishnamurthy, 2012. Intermediary Asset Pricing. Mimeo, Northwestern University.

[24] He. Z., Khang I. and A. Krishnamurthy,2010, Balance Sheet Adjustments during the 2008 Crisis, IMF Economic Review,58, 118–156

[25] Holmstrom, B. and J. Tirole, 1997. Financial Intermediation, Loanable Funds, and the Real Sector. Quarterly Journal of Economics 112, 663-692

[26] IMF, October 2014 Global Financial Stability Report

[27] Kiyotaki, N., and Moore, J., 1997. Credit Cycles. Journal of Political Economy 105, 211-248.

[28] Meh, Cesaire A. and Kevin Moran (2010) "The role of bank capital in the propagation of shocks," Journal of Economic Dynamics and Control, Vol. 34, pp. 555–576.

[29] Ordonez, G., 2013, Sustainable Shadow Banking, mimeo, University of Pennsylvania

[30] Parlatore, C. (2013), "Fragility in Money Market Funds: Sponsor Support and Regulation", mimeo, the Wharton School, University of Pennsylvania

[31] Pennacchi, George G, 1988. " Loan Sales and the Cost of Bank Capital," Journal of Finance, American Finance Association, vol. 43(2), pages 375-96, June.

[32] Plantin, G. 2012. "Shadow Banking and Bank Capital Regulation."Working Paper, Toulouse School of Economics.

[33] Poznar, Zoltan, Tobias Adrian, Adam Ashcraft, and Hayley Boesky. 2012. "Shadow Banking." Federal Reserve Bank of New York, Staff Report No. 458.

[34] Sufi , A. ,2007. "Informational Asymmetry and Financing Arrangements: Evidence from Syndicated Loans", Journal of Finance 62:629-668.

8 Appendix

In this appendix I derive the optimal contracts for three different scenarios regarding the observability of projects characteristics. A frictionless scenario in which both the ex-post outcome and the ex-ante quality of projects are observable. Then I derive the optimal contract for traditional banks, when the outcome of the project is not observable. And finally I solve the optimal contract for the shadow bank, when the outcome of the project is observable but the ex-ante quality is not.

In particular these results hold for a generic increasing linear function $\pi(e_t) = \kappa_1 e_t + \kappa_2$ and a convex quadratic cost function $c(e_t) = \tau_1 e_t^2 + \tau_2 e_t + \tau_3$. In the paper I assume $\kappa_1 = 1, \kappa_2 = 0$ and $\tau_3 = 0$.

8.1 Optimal Contract in the First Best Scenario

As explained in the main text, the optimal contract solves

$$\max Q_t k_t \left\{ E_t \Lambda_{t,t+1} \left[\pi_t \left(e_t^{fb} \right) \left(\bar{\theta}^G R_{t+1}^k - b_{t+1}^{G,fb} \right) + (1 - \pi_t(e_t)) \left(\bar{\theta}^b R_{t+1}^k - b_{t+1}^{B,fb} \right) \right] - c \left(e_t^{fb} \right) \right\}$$

$$Q_t k_t - n_t \leq E_t \Lambda_{t,t+1} \left[\pi_t \left(e_t^{fb} \right) b_{t+1}^g + (1 - \pi_t \left(e_t^{fb} \right)) b_{t+1}^b \right] Q_t k_t \quad (\mu_t)$$

$$b_{t+1}^{G,fb} \leq \bar{\theta}^G R_{t+1}^k \quad (\chi_{t+1}^g)$$

$$b_{t+1}^{B,fb} \leq \bar{\theta}^B R_{t+1}^k \quad (\chi_{t+1}^b)$$

The FOCs for $e_t^{fb}, k_t, b_{t+1}^g, b_{t+1}^b$ are

$$c'(e_t) = \pi'(e_t) E_t \Lambda_{t,t+1} \left[\bar{\Delta} R_{t+1}^k - \left(b_{t+1}^g - b_{t+1}^b \right) \right] + \pi'(e_t) \mu_t E_t \Lambda_{t,t+1} \left(b_{t+1}^g - b_{t+1}^b \right)$$

$$E_t \Lambda_{t,t+1} \left\{ \pi_t(e_t) \left(\bar{\theta}^g R_{t+1}^k - b_{t+1}^g \right) + (1 - \pi_t(e_t)) \left(\bar{\theta}^b R_{t+1}^k - b_{t+1}^b \right) \right\} - c(e_t) = \mu_t \left\{ 1 - E_t \Lambda_{t,t+1} \left[\pi_t(e_t) b_{t+1}^g + (1 - \pi_t(e_t) \right. \right.$$

$$\Lambda_{t,t+1} \pi_t(e_t) (\mu_t - 1) = \chi_{t+1}^g$$

$$\Lambda_{t,t+1} (1 - \pi_t(e_t)) (\mu_t - 1) = \chi_{t+1}^b$$

From the last two equations we see that either χ_{t+1}^G and χ_{t+1}^B are both positive or they are both zero. However if they were both positive the bank would not be obtaining any payoff from funding the projects. As a result $\chi_{t+1}^g = 0$ and $\chi_{t+1}^b = 0$, so that the main equations become

$$c' \left(e_t^{fb} \right) = \pi' \left(e_t^{fb} \right) E_t \Lambda_{t,t+1} \bar{\Delta} R_{t+1}^k$$

$$E_t \Lambda_{t,t+1} \left\{ \pi \left(e_t^{fb} \right) \bar{\theta}^g R_{t+1}^k + (1 - \pi \left(e_t^{fb} \right)) \bar{\theta}^b R_{t+1}^k \right\} - c \left(e_t^{fb} \right) = 1$$

$$\mu_t = 1$$

where I used $E_t \Lambda_{t,t+1} R_{t+1} = 1$. The first two equations are the same as (6) and (7) in the main text, whereas the last equation simply states that in the first best the marginal value of a unit of net worth is equal to one.

8.2 Optimal Contract for the Traditional Bank

As explained in the paper, the one period contract for the traditional bank will be given by the solution of the following

$$\max_{k_t^{tb}, e_t^{tb}, b_{t+1}^{tb}} Q_t k_t^{tb} \left\{ E_t \Lambda_{t,t+1} \left[\pi \left(e_t^{tb} \right) \bar{\theta}^G R_{t+1}^k + (1 - \pi \left(e_t^{tb} \right)) \bar{\theta}^B R_{t+1}^k - b_{t+1}^{tb} \right] - c \left(e_t^{tb} \right) \right\}$$

$$b_{t+1} \leq \theta_L R_{t+1}^k \ (IC) \ (\omega_{t+1})$$

$$\left(Q_t k_t^{tb} - n_t^{tb} \right) \leq E_t \Lambda_{t,t+1} b_{t+1} Q_t k_t^{tb} \ (PC) \ \left(\lambda_t^{tb} \right)$$

The first order conditions with respect to $k_t^{tb}, b_{t+1}^{tb}, e_t^{tb}$ are

$$E_t \Lambda_{t,t+1} \left[\Theta_{t+1}(e_t^{tb}) R_{t+1}^k - b_{t+1}^{tb} \right] - c(\pi_t^{tb}) - \lambda_t^{tb} \left[1 - E_t \Lambda_{t+1} b_{t+1}^{tb} \right] = 0 \tag{45}$$

$$Q_t k_t^{tb} \Lambda_{t+1} \left[\lambda_t^{tb} - 1 \right] = \omega_{t+1} \tag{46}$$

$$c'(e_t^{tb}) = \pi'(e_t^{tb}) E_t \Lambda_{t+1} \bar{\Delta}_{t+1} R_{t+1}^k \tag{47}$$

where ω_{t+1} and λ_t^{tb} are the Lagrange multipliers on the incentive constraint and the participation constraint.

The last equation directly determines the screening level for traditional banks, as reported above. In addition, from (46), we see that the SC will bind if $\lambda_t^{tb} - 1 > 0$, a condition that we assume to hold in a neighborhood of the steady state.

Then, substituting the incentive constraint into (45) this condition can be rewritten as

$$\lambda_t^{tb} = \frac{E_t \Lambda_{t,t+1} \left[\Theta_{t+1}(e_t^{tb}) R_{t+1}^k - \theta_L R_{t+1}^k \right] - c(e_t^{tb})}{1 - \theta_L E_t \Lambda_{t+1} R_{t+1}^k} > 1$$

which implies

$$\frac{E_t \Lambda_{t,t+1} \left[\Theta_{t+1}(e_t^{tb}) R_{t+1}^k - R_{t+1} \right] - c(e_t^{tb})}{1 - \theta_L E_t \Lambda_{t+1} R_{t+1}^k} > 0$$

that indicates how the incentive constraint for the traditional bank implies a wedge between the expected return on capital and the risk-free rate.

Finally, we can combine the (IC) the (PC) in order to obtain an expression for the leverage ratio reported in (11)

$$Q_t k_t^{tb} = \frac{1}{\left[1 - \theta_L E_t \Lambda_{t+1} R_{t+1}^k \right]} n_t^{tb} = \phi_t^{tb} n_t^{tb}$$

In addition from the PC we can think of the face value of the debt raised by the TB as being given by

$$R_{t+1}^{TB} = \frac{b_{t+1}^{tb} Q_t k_t^{tb}}{\left(Q_t k_t^{tb} - n_t^{tb} \right)} = \theta^L R_{t+1}^k \frac{\phi_t}{\phi_t - 1}$$

8.3 Optimal Contract for the Shadow Bank

In this section I report the complet solution to the problem to the optimal contract of the shadow bank. As explained in the paper, the problem to be solved is the following:

$$\max_{k_t^{sb},e_t^{sb},b_{t+1}^{g,sb},b_{t+1}^{b,sb}} Q_t k_t \left\{ E_t \Lambda_{t,t+1} \left[\pi \left(e_t^{sb}\right) \left(\bar{\theta}^G R_{t+1}^k - b_{t+1}^{G,sb}\right) + (1 - \pi\left(e_t^{sb}\right)) \left(\bar{\theta}^B R_{t+1}^k - b_{t+1}^{B,sb}\right) \right] - c\left(e_t^{sb}\right) \right\}$$

$$R_{t+1} \left(Q_t k_t - n_t\right) \leq \left[\pi \left(e_t^{sb}\right) b_{t+1}^{G,sb} + (1 - \pi\left(e_t^{sb}\right)) b_{t+1}^{B,sb} \right] Q_t k_t \quad (\mu_{t+1}) \quad \text{(PC)}$$

$$c' \left(e_t^{sb}\right) \leq \pi' \left(e_t^{sb}\right) E_t \Lambda_{t,t+1} \left[\bar{\Delta} R_{t+1}^k - \left(b_{t+1}^{G,sb} - b_{t+1}^{B,sb}\right) \right] \quad (\rho_t) \quad \text{(IC)}$$

$$b_{t+1}^{G,sb} \leq \bar{\theta}^G R_{t+1}^k \quad \left(\chi_{t+1}^g\right) \quad \text{(LL)}$$

$$b_{t+1}^{B,sb} \leq \bar{\theta}^B R_{t+1}^k \quad \left(\chi_{t+1}^b\right) \quad \text{(LL)}$$

where $\mu_{t+1}, \rho_t, \chi_{t+1}^g$ and χ_{t+1}^b are the multipliers associated with each constraint. The implied FOCs are

$$e_t^{sb} : c'\left(e_t^{sb}\right) = \pi'\left(e_t^{sb}\right) E_t \Lambda_{t,t+1} \left[\bar{\Delta} R_{t+1}^k - \left(b_{t+1}^{G,sb} - b_{t+1}^{B,sb}\right) \right] + \pi'\left(e_t^{sb}\right) E_t \mu_{t+1} \left(b_{t+1}^{G,sb} - b_{t+1}^{B,sb}\right) - \rho_t c''\left(e_t^{sb}\right)$$

$$k_t : \quad E_t \Lambda_{t,t+1} \left\{ \pi_t\left(e_t^{sb}\right) \left(\bar{\theta}^G R_{t+1}^k - b_{t+1}^g\right) + (1 - \pi_t\left(e_t^{sb}\right)) \left(\bar{\theta}^B R_{t+1}^k - b_{t+1}^b\right) \right\} - c\left(e_t^{sb}\right) =$$
$$E_t \mu_{t+1} \left\{ R_{t+1} - \left[\pi_t\left(e_t^{sb}\right) b_{t+1}^g + (1 - \pi_t\left(e_t^{sb}\right)) b_{t+1}^b \right] \right\}$$

$$b_{t+1}^{G,sb} : \rho_t \pi'\left(e_t^{sb}\right) \Lambda_{t,t+1} = \pi_t\left(e_t^{sb}\right) \left(\mu_{t+1} - \Lambda_{t,t+1}\right) - \chi_{t+1}^g$$

$$b_{t+1}^{B,sb} : \quad \rho_t \pi'\left(e_t^{sb}\right) \Lambda_{t,t+1} = \chi_{t+1}^b - (1 - \pi_t\left(e_t^{sb}\right)) \left(\mu_{t+1} - \Lambda_{t,t+1}\right)$$

$$\mu_{t+1} : R_{t+1} \left(\phi_t^{sb} - 1\right) = \left[\pi_t\left(e_t^{sb}\right) b_{t+1}^{G,sb} + (1 - \pi_t\left(e_t^{sb}\right)) b_{t+1}^{B,sb} \right] \phi_t^{sb}$$

$$\rho_t : \quad c'\left(e_t^{sb}\right) = \pi'\left(e_t^{sb}\right) E_t \Lambda_{t,t+1} \left[\bar{\Delta} R_{t+1}^k - \left(b_{t+1}^{G,sb} - b_{t+1}^{B,sb}\right) \right]$$

where in the first equation I have used that $\pi''\left(e_t\right) = 0$.

First notice that if $\rho_t > 0$ then it can't be that $\chi_{t+1}^g = 0$ and $\chi_{t+1}^b = 0$ otherwise this would imply $\left(\mu_{t+1} - \Lambda_{t,t+1}\right) = 0$ and then $\rho_t = 0$, a contradiction, therefore at least one of the two payment has to be at the maximum. In addition, setting both payments to the maximum would not be optimal since it would imply that the bank does not receive any payoff, so that only one limited liability constraint can be binding.

In particular, by combining the first order conditions for $b_{t+1}^{G,sb}$ and $b_{t+1}^{B,sb}$ it can be seen that the only case compatible with $\rho_t > 0$ is $\chi_{t+1}^g = 0$ and $\chi_{t+1}^b > 0 \implies b_{t+1}^{B,sb} \leq \bar{\theta}^b R_{t+1}^k$, the intuition being that setting $b_{t+1}^{B,sb}$ to its maximum improves on the incentive constraint on monitoring.

As a result, the FOCs for $b_{t+1}^{G,sb}$ implies

$$\mu_{t+1} = \Lambda_{t,t+1} \left[\rho_t \frac{\pi'\left(e_t^{sb}\right)}{\pi\left(e_t^{sb}\right)} + 1 \right] \tag{48}$$

and if we substitute this relationship in the FOC for k_t^{sb} we obtain

$$\left\{ E_t \Lambda_{t,t+1} \left[\Theta_{t+1}\left(e_t^{sb}\right) R_{t+1}^k - R_{t+1} \right] - c\left(e_t^{sb}\right) \right\} = \rho_t \frac{\pi'\left(e_t^{sb}\right)}{\pi\left(e_t^{sb}\right)} \frac{1}{\phi_t^{sb}} \tag{49}$$

where $\phi_t^{sb} = Q_t k_t^{sb} / n_t^{sb}$.

Therefore, when the (IC) binds there will be a positive spread between the expected return on capital and the risk-free rate, as indicated by equation (21).

In addition, if the (IC) binds then we can rewrite the FOC for e_t and the incentive constraint as

$$\rho_t c'' \left(e_t^{sb}\right) = \pi' \left(e_t^{sb}\right) E_t \mu_{t+1} \left(b_{t+1}^{G,sb} - \bar{\theta}^B R_{t+1}^k\right)$$

$$c' \left(e_t^{sb}\right) = \pi' \left(e_t^{sb}\right) E_t \Lambda_{t,t+1} \left[\bar{\theta}^G R_{t+1}^k - b_{t+1}^{G,sb}\right]$$

From the first equation we see that if $\rho_t > 0$ then $E_t \mu_{t+1} \left(b_{t+1}^{G,sb} - \bar{\theta}^b R_{t+1}^k\right) > 0$, and because of (48) this also implies $E_t \Lambda_{t,t+1} \left(b_{t+1}^{G,sb} - \bar{\theta}^B R_{t+1}^k\right) > 0$. As a result, if we rewrite the second equation as

$$c' \left(e_t\right) = E_t \Lambda_{t,t+1} \bar{\Delta}_{t+1} R_{t+1}^k - E_t \Lambda_{t,t+1} \left(b_{t+1}^{G,sb} - \bar{\theta}^B R_{t+1}^k\right)$$

you obtain equation (22)

$$c' \left(e_t^{sb}\right) < E_t \Lambda_{t,t+1} \bar{\Delta}_{t+1} R_{t+1}^k$$

This is an important relationship since it implies that the screening effort of shadow banks is lower than the one of traditional banks, so that

$$\pi(e_t^{sb}) < \pi(e_t^{tb}) \tag{50}$$

Next, from the (PC) we can obtain the payment to the bank in the good state

$$b_{t+1}^{G,sb} = \frac{1}{\pi(e_t^{sb})} \left[R_{t+1} \frac{\left(\phi_t^{sb} - 1\right)}{\phi_t^{sb}} - (1 - \pi_t \left(e_t^{sb}\right))\bar{\theta}^B R_{t+1}^k\right] \tag{51}$$

and by substituting this in the (IC) we obtain the leverage constraint reported in the main text

$$\phi_t^{sb} \leq \frac{\pi' \left(e_t^{sb}\right))}{\left\{\pi_t \left(e_t^{sb}\right) c' \left(e_t^{sb}\right) - \pi' \left(e_t^{sb}\right) \left[E_t \Lambda_{t,t+1} \Theta_{t+1} \left(e_t^{sb}\right) R_{t+1}^k - 1\right]\right\}} \tag{52}$$

Finally, substituting (48) and (51) in the FOC for e_t^{sb} one obtains

$$\rho_t c''(e_t^{sb}) = \pi' \left(e_t^{sb}\right)) \left[\rho_t \frac{\pi' \left(e_t^{sb}\right)}{\pi \left(e_t^{sb}\right)} + 1\right] E_t \Lambda_{t,t+1} \left(b_{t+1}^G - \bar{\theta}^B R_{t+1}^k\right)$$

and by using the (IC) at equality

$$\rho_t c'' \left(e_t^{sb}\right) = \pi' \left(e_t^{sb}\right) \left[\rho_t \frac{\pi' \left(e_t^{sb}\right)}{\pi \left(e_t^{sb}\right)} + 1\right] \left[E_t \Lambda_{t,t+1} \bar{\Delta}_{t+1} R_{t+1}^k - c' \left(e_t^{sb}\right))\right]$$

Finally if we substitute for ρ_t^{sb} from (49) we obtain the equation determining e_t^{sb}

$$\left[\pi' \left(e_t^{sb}\right) E \Lambda_{t,t+1} \bar{\Delta} R_{t+1}^k - c' \left(e_t^{sb}\right)\right] \left\{\pi_t \left(e_t^{sb}\right) c' \left(e_t^{sb}\right) - \pi'_t \left(e_t^{sb}\right) c \left(e_t^{sb}\right)\right\} = \tag{53}$$

$$\left\{E_t \Lambda_{t,t+1} \left[\Theta \left(e_t^{sb}\right) R_{t+1}^k - R_{t+1}\right] - c \left(e_t^{sb}\right)\right\} \left[\pi_t \left(e_t^{sb}\right) c''(e_t^{sb})\right]$$

At this point, we can use such equation to study the determinants of e_t^{sb}.

Let's define

$$g(e_t^{sb}, E_t \Lambda_{t,t+1} R_{t+1}^k) = \left\{ E_t \Lambda_{t,t+1} \Theta_{t+1} \left(e_t^{sb} \right) R_{t+1}^k - 1 - c \left(e_t^{sb} \right) \right\} \left[\pi_t \left(e_t^{sb} \right) c'' \left(e_t^{sb} \right) \right]$$

$$- \left[\pi' \left(e_t \right) E \Lambda_{t,t+1} \bar{\Delta} R_{t+1}^k - c' \left(e_t^{sb} \right) \right] \left\{ \pi_t \left(e_t^{sb} \right) c' \left(e_t^{sb} \right) - \pi_t' \left(e_t^{sb} \right) c \left(e_t^{sb} \right) \right\} = 0$$

Therefore we can obtain

$$\begin{aligned}
\frac{dg}{de_t^{sb}} &= \left[\pi' \left(e_t^{sb} \right) c'' \left(e_t^{sb} \right) + \pi_t \left(e_t^{sb} \right) c''' \left(e_t^{sb} \right) \right] \left\{ E_t \Lambda_{t,t+1} \Theta \left(e_t^{sb} \right) R_{t+1}^k - 1 - c \left(e_t^{sb} \right) \right\} \\
&\quad + c'' \left(e_t^{sb} \right) \left\{ \pi_t \left(e_t^{sb} \right) c' \left(e_t^{sb} \right) - \pi_t' \left(e_t^{sb} \right) c \left(e_t^{sb} \right) \right\} > 0
\end{aligned}$$

Given (49), and the fact that $\pi_t \left(e_t^{sb} \right) c' \left(e_t^{sb} \right) - \pi_t' \left(e_t^{sb} \right) c \left(e_t^{sb} \right) \geq 0$ since this quantity is proportional to the objective of the banker when the constraint binds, then, as long as $c''' \left(e_t^{sb} \right) \geq 0$ (as it is implied by the cost function we use) we have that $\frac{dg}{de_t^{sb}} > 0$.

In addition,

$$\begin{aligned}
\frac{dg}{dE_t \Lambda_{t,t+1} R_{t+1}^k} &= \pi_t \left(e_t^{sb} \right) c'' \left(e_t^{sb} \right) E_t \Theta_{t+1} \left(e_t^{sb} \right) - \pi' \left(e_t^{sb} \right) E_t \bar{\Delta}_{t+1} \left\{ \pi_t \left(e_t^{sb} \right) c' \left(e_t^{sb} \right) - \pi_t' \left(e_t^{sb} \right) c \left(e_t^{sb} \right) \right\} \\
&= \pi_t \left(e_t^{sb} \right) c'' \left(e_t^{sb} \right) E_t \bar{\theta}_{t+1}^B + E_t \bar{\Delta}_{t+1} c \left(e_t^{sb} \right) + \pi \left(e_t^{sb} \right) E_t \bar{\Delta}_{t+1} \left[\pi_t \left(e_t^{sb} \right) c'' \left(e_t^{sb} \right) - c' \left(e_t^{sb} \right) \right] > 0
\end{aligned}$$

where the term in the square brackets is positive for the class of cost functions that we consider.

At this point, if we employ the implicit function theorem we will have

$$\frac{de_t^{sb}}{dE_t \Lambda_{t,t+1} \bar{\Delta} R_{t+1}^k} = -\frac{dg/dE_t \Lambda_{t,t+1} \bar{\Delta} R_{t+1}^k}{dg/de_t^{sb}} < 0$$

so that the monitoring intensity of shadow banks will be decreasing in the expected return on capital.

Finally, if we use the cost function $c \left(e \right) = \frac{\tau}{2} \left(e^2 + \iota e \right)$ we obtain

$$\pi_t^{sb} = e_t^{sb} = 2 \frac{E_t \Lambda_{t,t+1} \left[R_{t+1} - \theta^B R_{t+1}^k \right]}{\left[E \Lambda_{t,t+1} \bar{\Delta}_{t+1} R_{t+1}^k - \frac{\tau}{2} \iota \right]}$$

9 Tables and Figures

Table 1: Parameters

Parameter	Value	Description	Target
Conventional			
β	0.99	Discount rate	
η^{-1}	1	Frisch Elasticity	
χ	2	Labor Utility weight	
α	.36	Capital Share in Production	
δ	.025	Depreciation Rate	
f''	2.3	Elasticity of Price to Investments	
Bank-specific			Target
θ_H	1.036	High Idiosyncratic Realization	$\phi^{sb} = 12$
θ_L	0.747	Low Idiosyncratic Realization	$\phi^{tb} = 4$
p^G/p^B	1.6	Ratio of Success Rates	$R^k - R = .004$
ω^{tb}	.18	Transfer to Traditional Banks	$K^{tb}/K = .5$
ω^{sb}	.05	Transfer to Shadow Banks	$K^{sb}/K = .5$
σ	.9	Bankers survival probability	10qtr horizon
τ	.19	Monitoring Cost Parameter	$\pi^{sb} = .95$
ι	-.94	Monitoring Cost Parameter	$\pi^{tb} = .975$

Table 2: Steady State Values

	Baseline Model	Traditional Banking Economy	Frictionless Economy
	Steady State Values		
Q	1	1	1
Y	2.2390	2.0706	2.3234
C^h	1.7264	1.6659	1.7822
K	20.5062	17.1137	22.5962
$\hat{\Theta}$	1	1.0014	1.0011
K^{tb}/K	.5	1	
K^{sb}/K	.5		
ϕ^{tb}	4	4.0502	
ϕ^{sb}	12		
π^{tb}	.975	0.9771	
π^{sb}	.97		
$\hat{\pi}$	.9625	0.9771	0.9738
$R^k - R$	.004	.008	.002

Figure 3: TFP shock, 1% drop in A_t, persistence .95

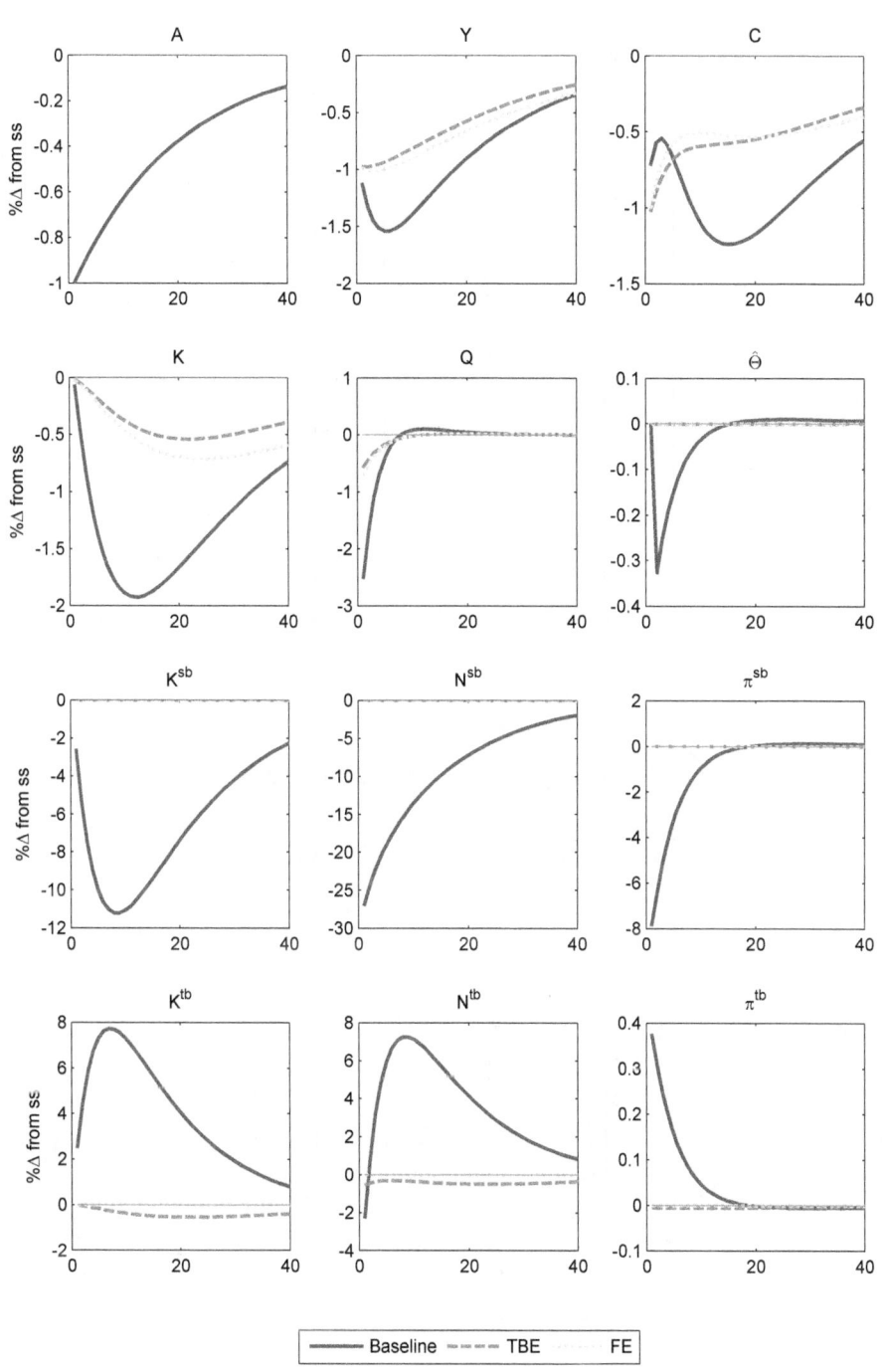

Figure 4: Subprime shock, 10% drop in $\bar{\theta}_t^B$

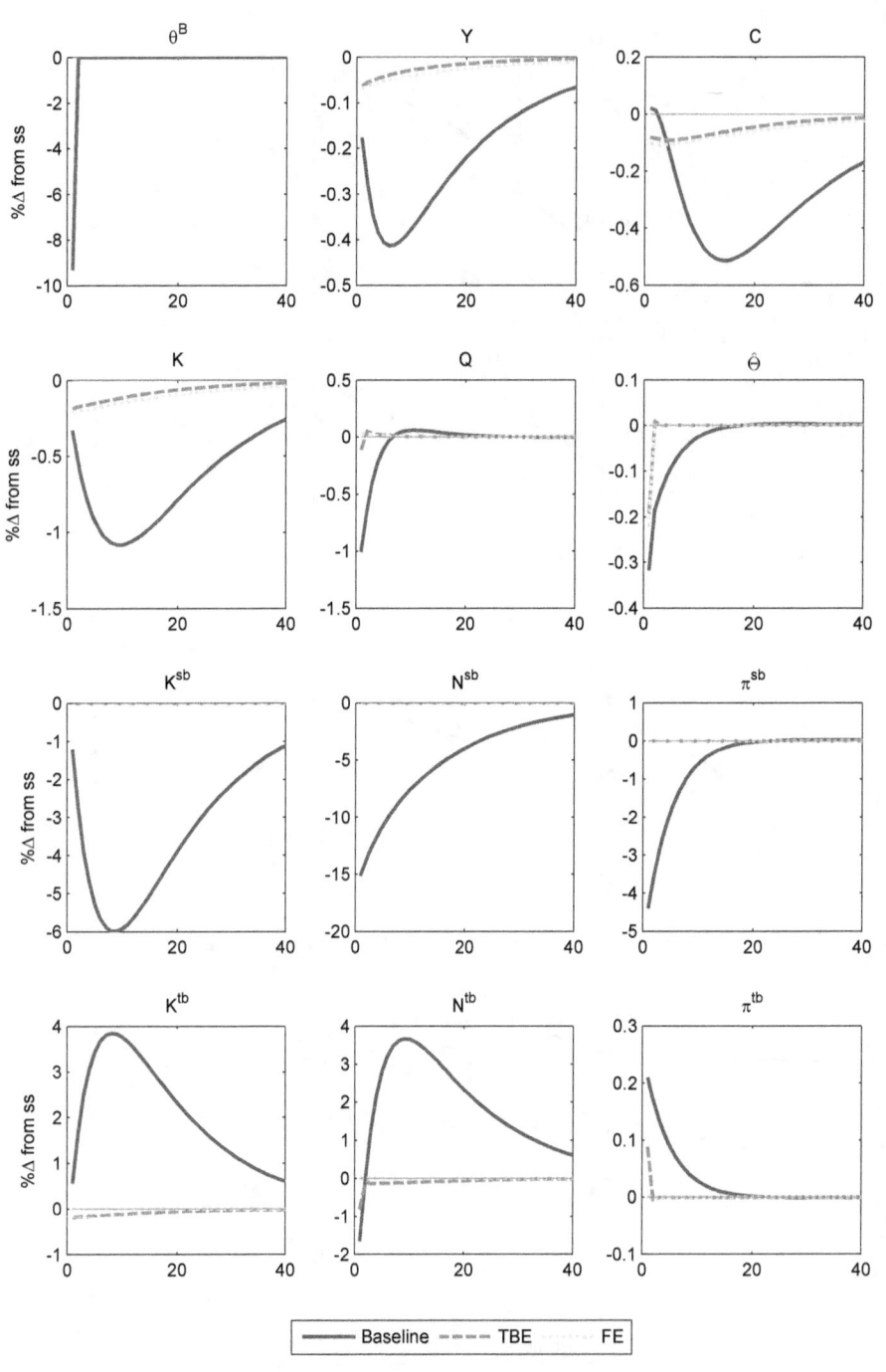

Figure 5: Cross-sectional standard deviation of equity returns

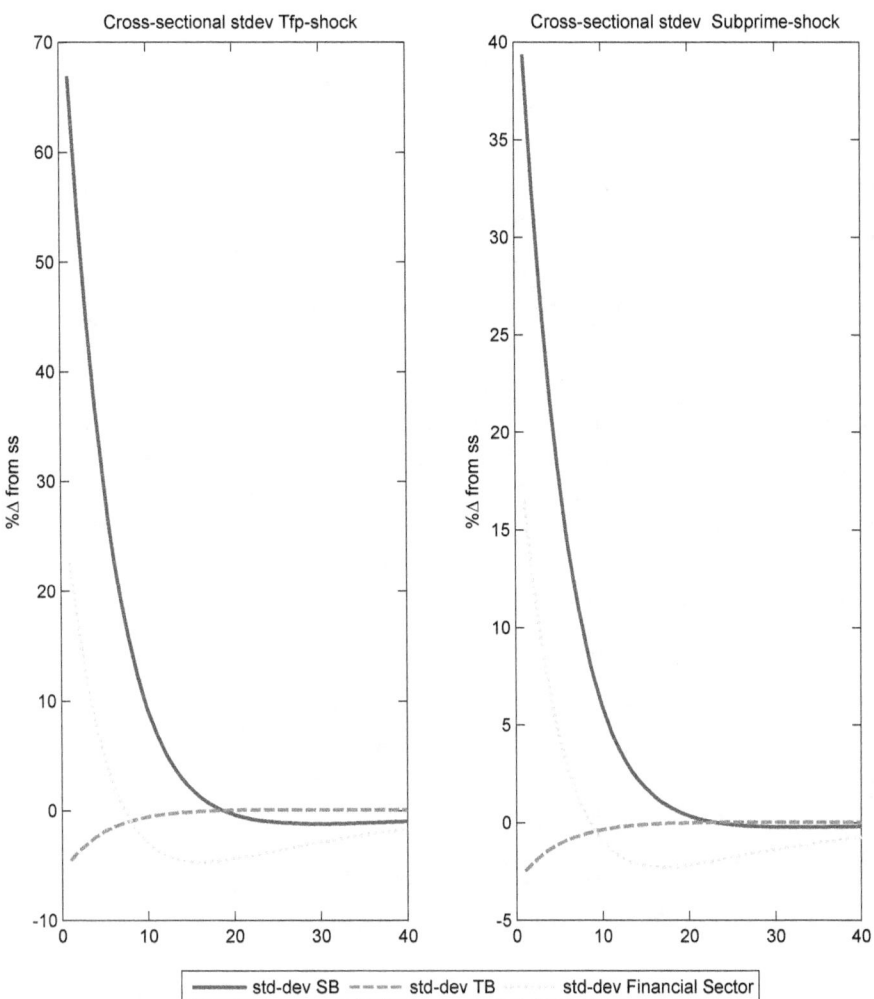

Figure 6: Screening cost shock, 5% increase in τ_t, peristence .5

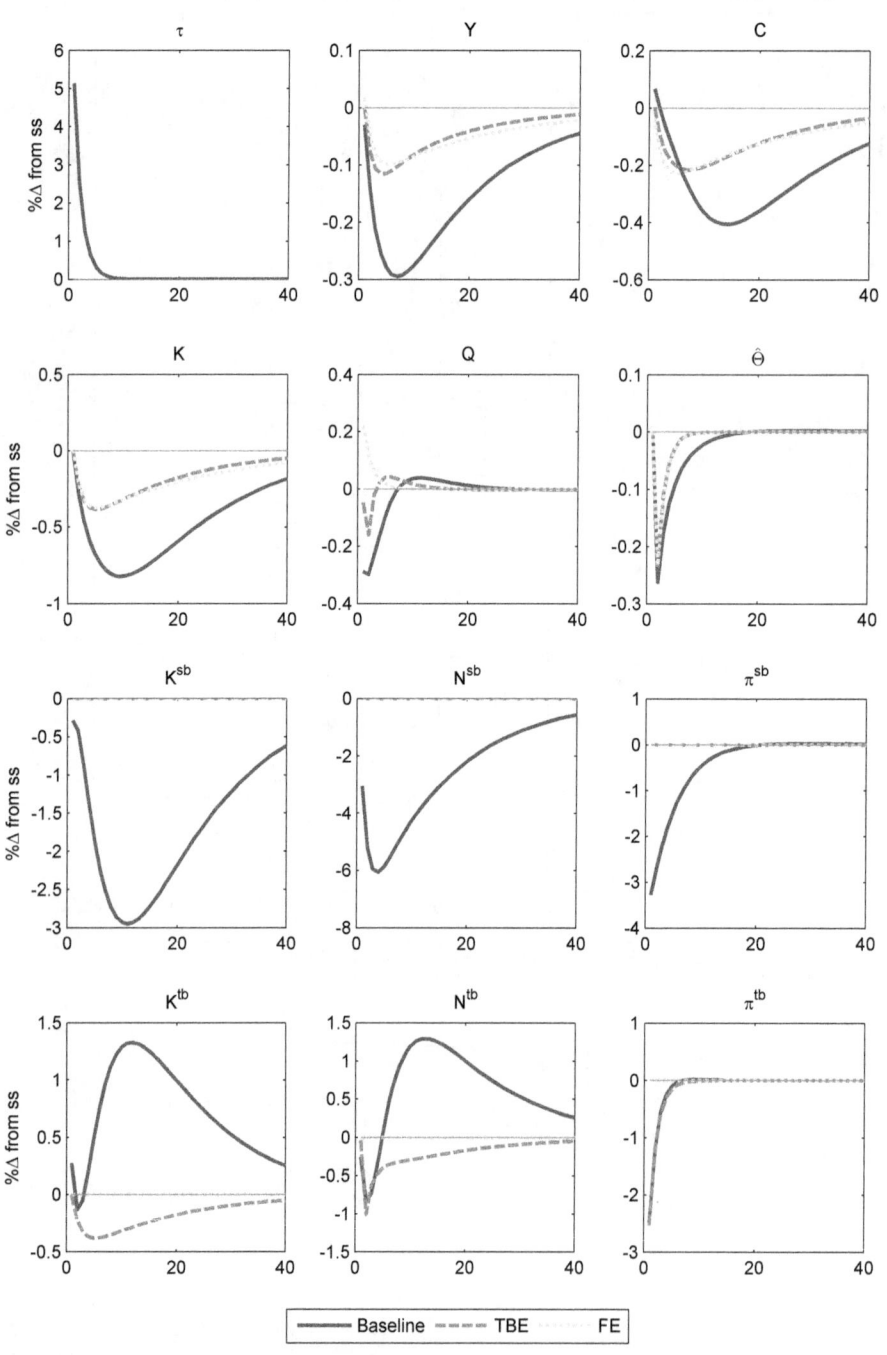

Figure 7: One time transfer from SB to TB equal to 1% of SB net worth

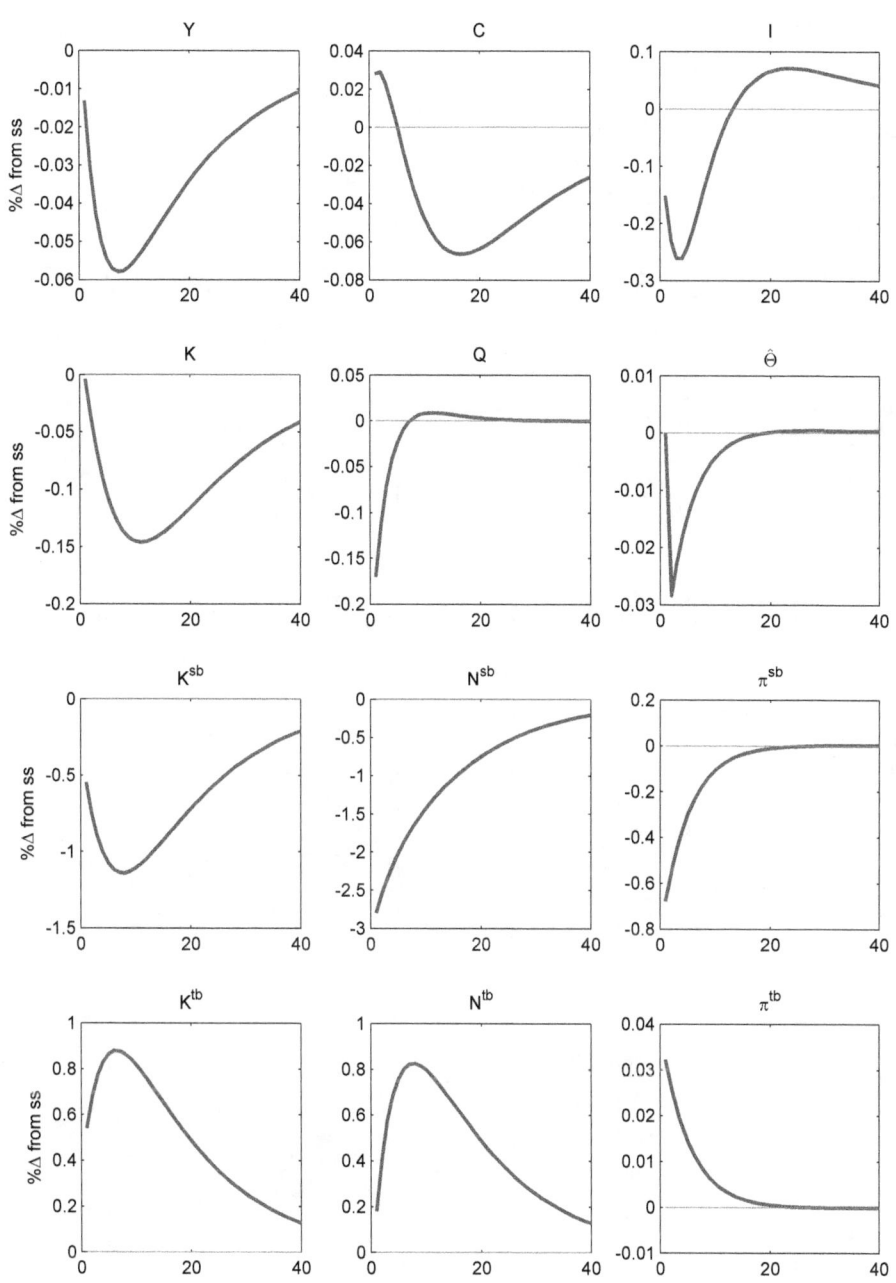

Figure 8: Run on the SB-system after a TFP shock

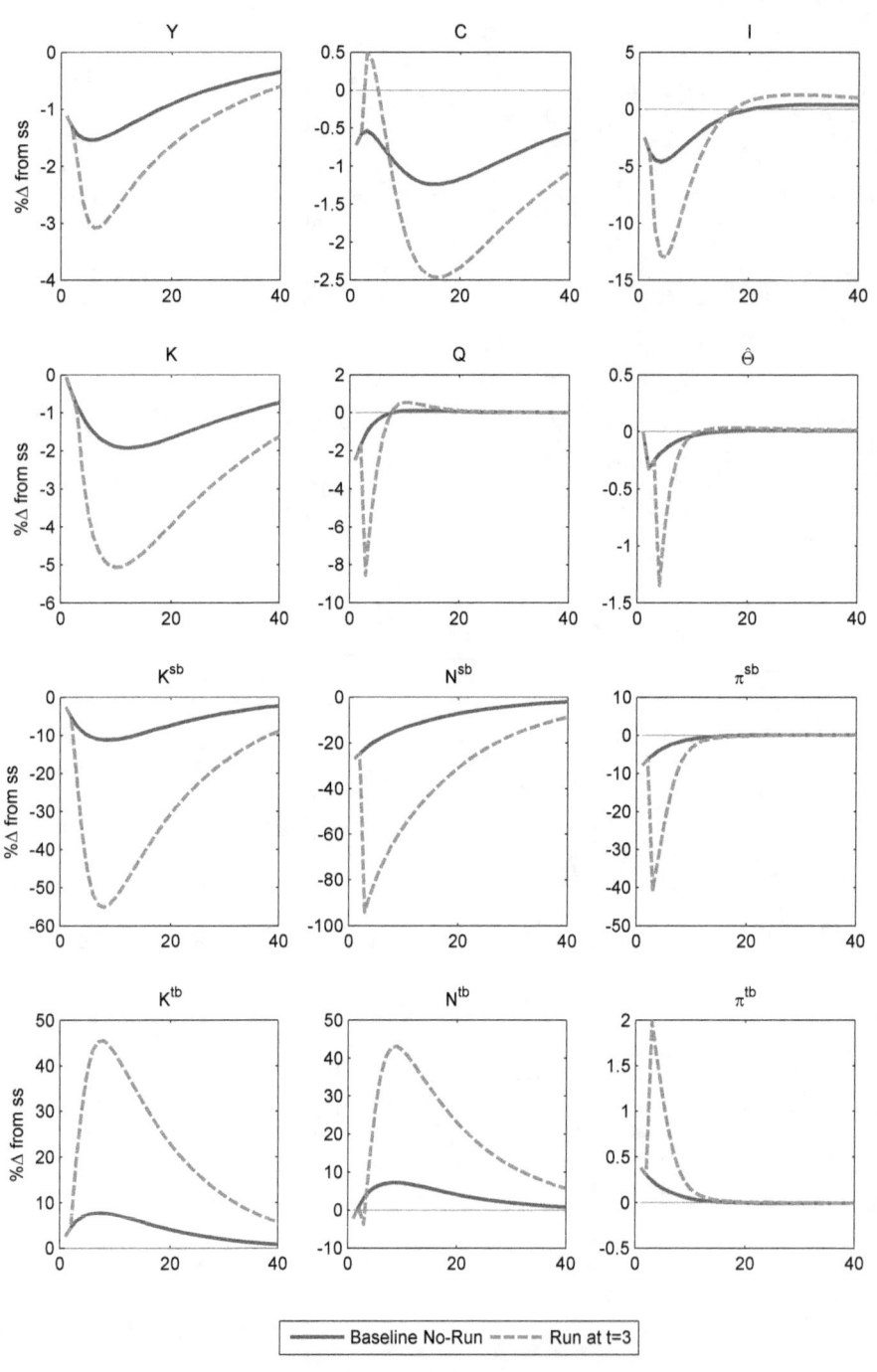

Figure 9: Run on the SB-system after a subprime shock

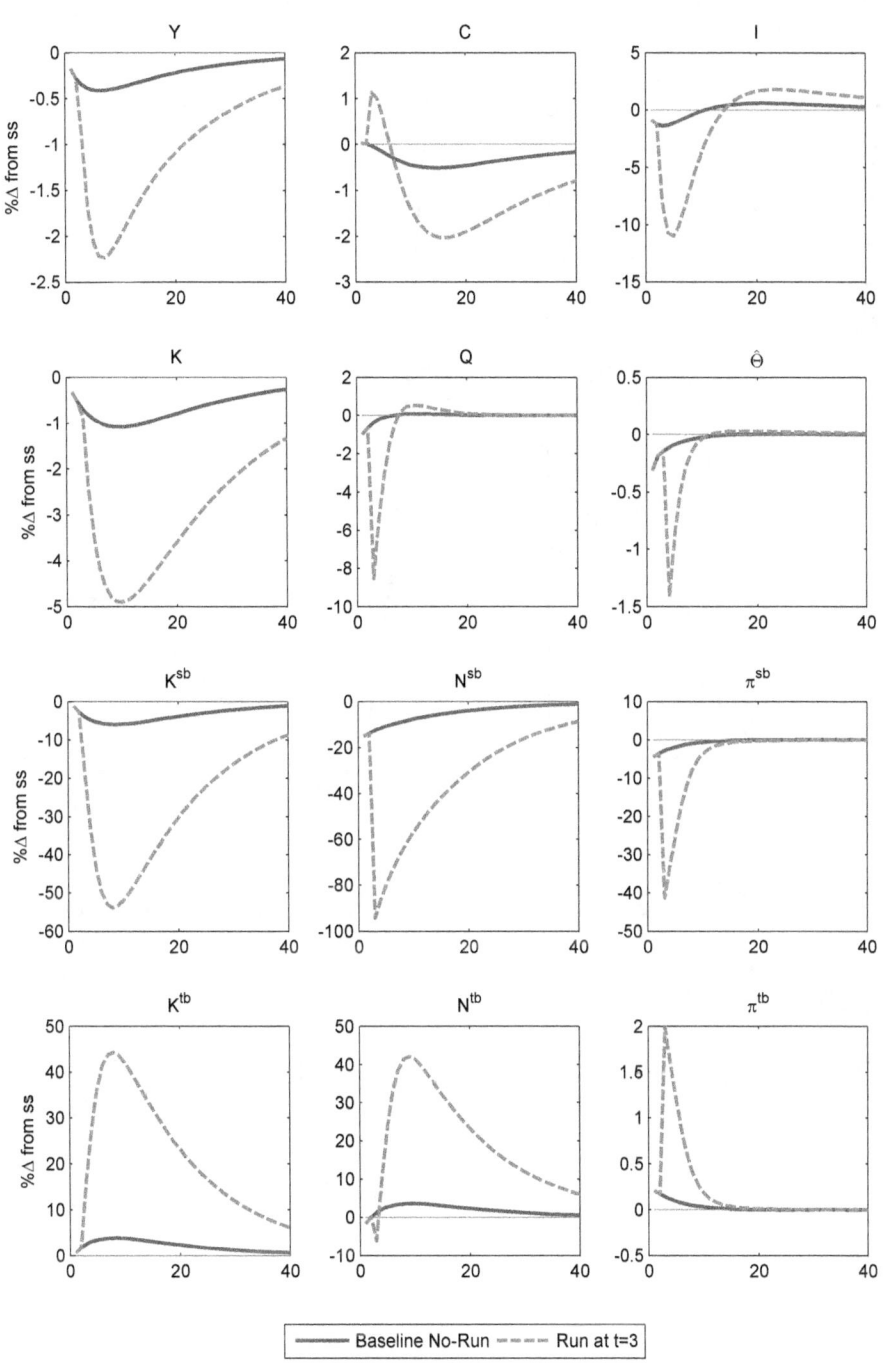

Figure 10: Run feasibility

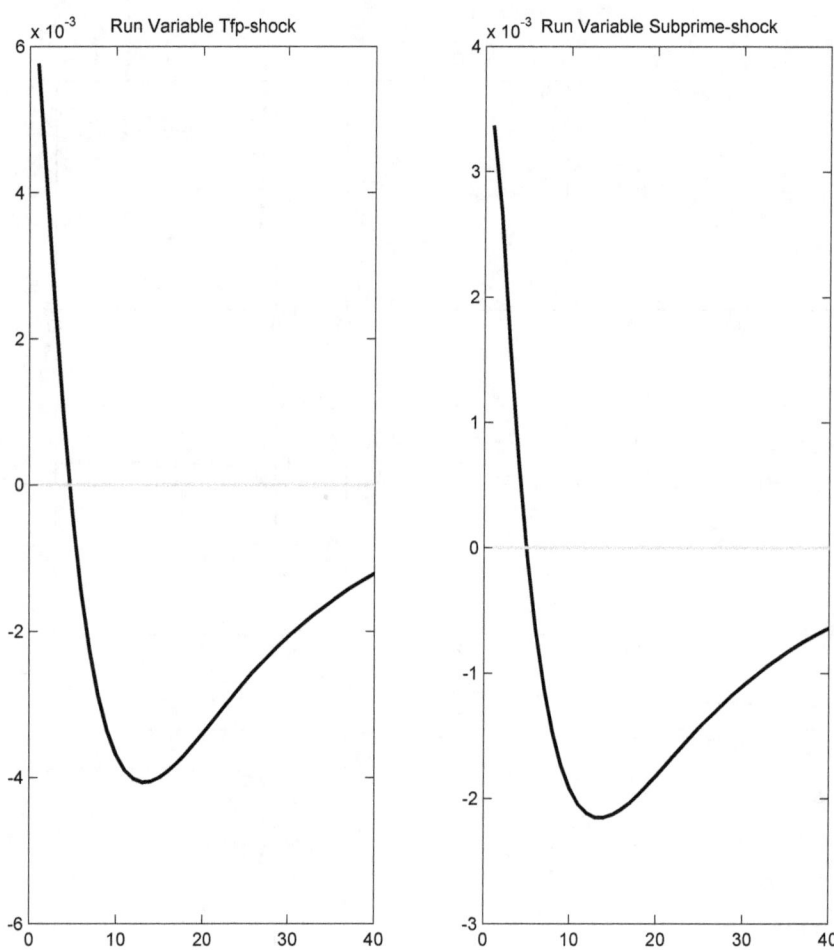

Figure 11: TFP shock and credit policy

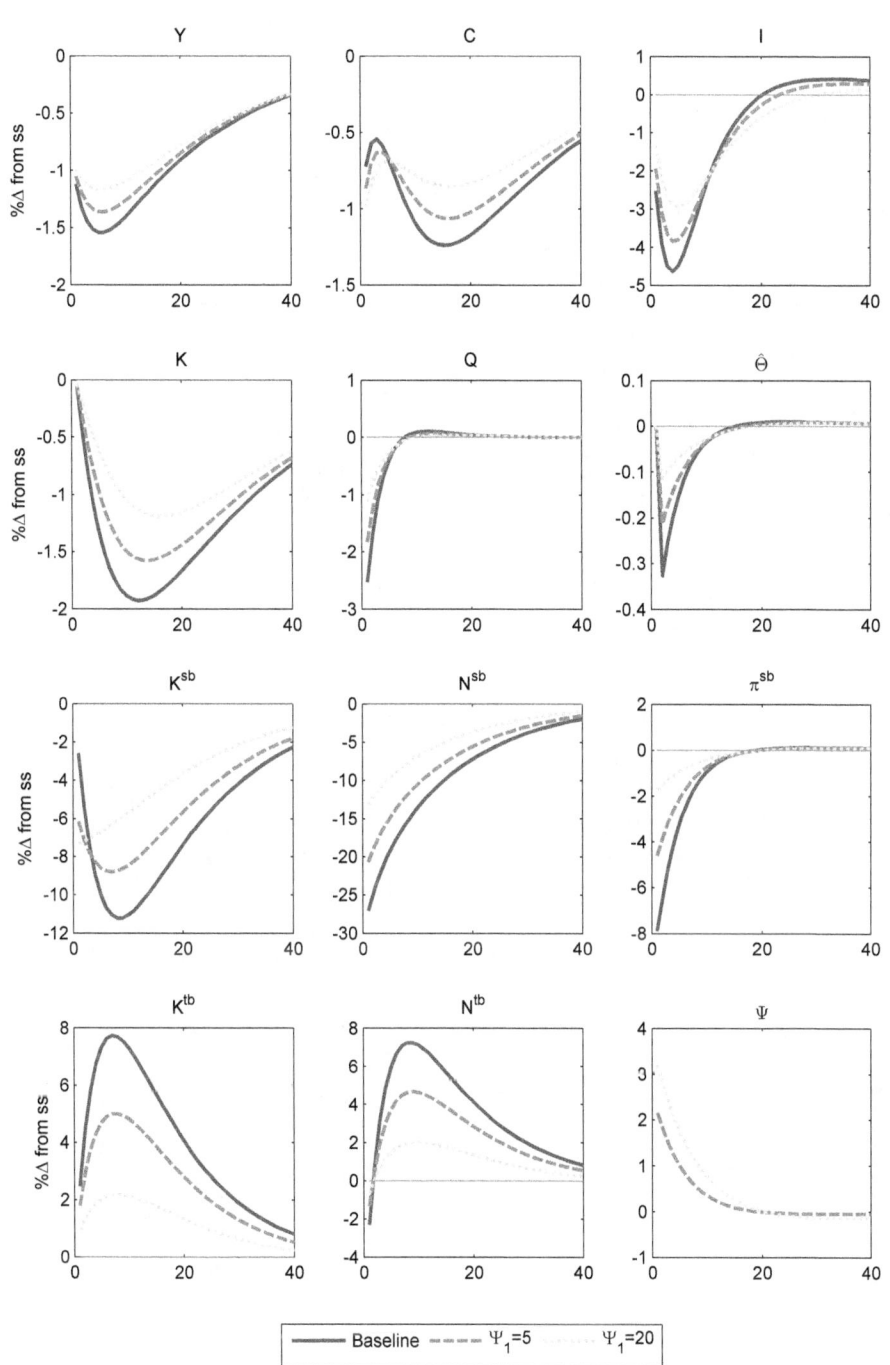

Figure 12: Subprime shock and credit policy

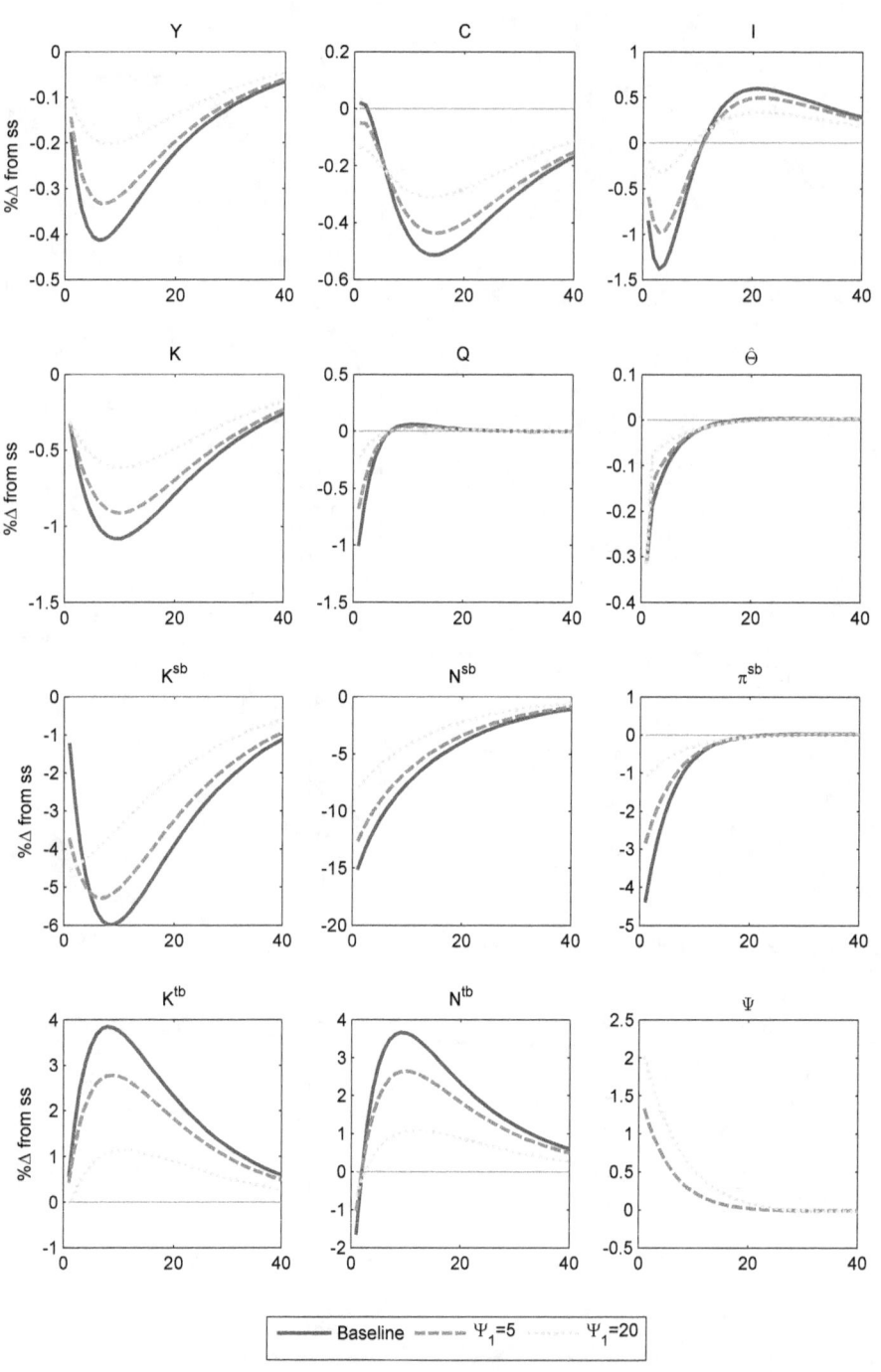

Figure 13: Fraction of "alert" investors necessary for a run ($\bar{\gamma}$) as government intervention Ψ_1 increases (TFP-shock on the left and subprime shock on the right)

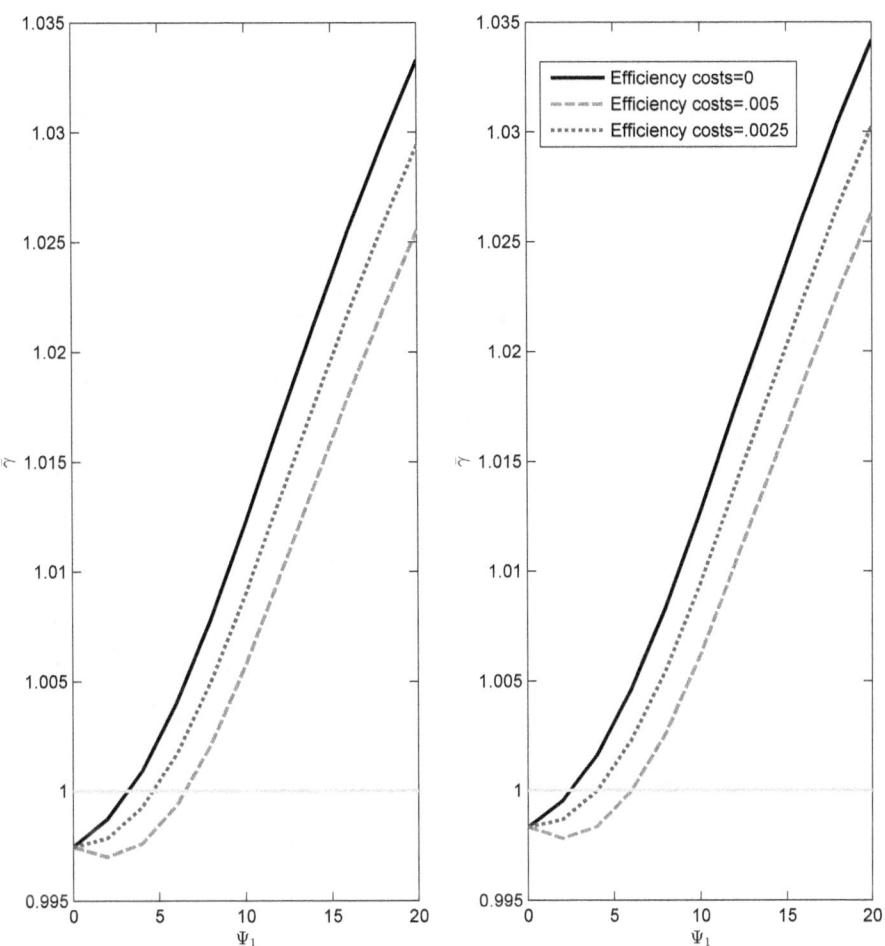